This magical Beyond The Sec parts in one po and could be the magic lamp for which you have been searching!

Read and learn how to...

Become A Magnet To Money

And learn how to raise your spiritual power of awareness through...

The Sea of Unlimited Consciousness

Become A Magnet To Money
by Bob Proctor and Michele Blood
Copyright © B. Proctor & M. Blood
February 14, 1995- March 05, 2008
MusiVation International Publishing

The Sea Of Unlimited Consciousness
by Michele Blood
Copyright © M. A Blood June 04, 2008
MusiVation International Publishing
(revised edition July 2012)

MusiVation International LLC
P O Box 12933
La Jolla California 92039
USA
All rights reserved.
Printed in the United States of America
ISBN: 978-1-533019-646
2nd edition April 2009

This book may not be copied, duplicated or used in any way without the written permission of the publishers.

Call 1 (858) 268-8688 for wholesale copies
of paperback and audio book versions.
Let your whole team study these power
Principles for Consciousness and Success!

Book Cover Photograph by Mayer George Vladimirovich
Cover Design by John Endara

Dedication

Part One of this book is dedicated to Dr. Wilma McIntyre who left her body in February 2008. Wilma was dedicated to learning, teaching and living the Universal Laws of Light. She helped so many wake up to their unlimited spiritual true self. She was a beautiful person and a beacon of Light and Love to all who knew her.

Thank you Wilma for your love, laughter, Light and unconditional friendship. May God continue to bless your soul greatly. Thank you for bringing more Light, joy and love to our world.

> Wilma we love you, you made a difference
> and your Light still shines on...

Part One
Become A Magnet To Money
TABLE OF CONTENTS

Dedication	3
What others are saying about this book	6
Introduction to parts one & two	9
Wealth and Happiness	14
Prosperity Consciousness	19
Stop Pressing the Same Buttons	22
Multiple Sources of Income (MSI's)	24
MSI Map	28
Providing Service	29
An Infinite Supply	32
The Law of Relativity & Income Acceleration	34
Renew your Marvelous Mind	37
The Power Of Decision	46
Persistence	52
Creative Visualization	57
The Power Of Meditation	63
Diagram of our amazing Mind	68
The Mind	69
The Terror Barrier Diagram	73
The Terror Barrier	74
The Power of a daily Action List	79
My Daily List	84
Responsibility	86
Gratitude & Appreciation	88
What is Consciousness?	90
Intuition	93
The Pole of Prosperity	99
New Life Letter	103

Part Two
The Sea Of Unlimited Consciousness
TABLE OF CONTENTS

Enter The Sea Of Unlimited Consciousness	104
Dedication & Thanks	105
The Sea Of Unlimited Consciousness	106
Levels Into The Sea of Unlimited Consciousness	110
Level One: The Human Experience	118
Level Two: I am more than my body	123
How to find a Teacher	138
Level Three: Our Soul Connection	141
Level Four: Becoming Mermaid/Man	160
Sex & Relationships	169
How do we know who is a Level Four?	180
Level FIVE: I AM THE SEA	194
Highly Recommended	203
Books by Enlightened Masters	210

What others are saying about this book...

I have been blessed to have the opportunity to speak to and work with spiritual seekers all over the world and there has always been a common thread that unites all of us: The questions, who are we, and why are we here? In this volume the authors masterly address those questions by allowing us to explore what level we are experiencing in relationship to our spiritual path and prosperity consciousness. They provide a spiritual blueprint to move from darkness into the Light using their own personal experiences. This complete volume is a must read for anyone seeking to live a vibrant, fulfilled, abundant life full of joy, higher consciousness, and love.
Lawrence T. Bond, PhD, RScP

It changed my life. Great book, with a holistic approach to success and abundance. In my life as a scientist and also as a teacher of eastern philosophy I found this to be the most simple explanation of great, timeless, spiritual truths about success and consciousness.
Nandini V. Katre, Ph.D. award winning scientist and author of "What's Science Got To Do With It"

The 2nd half of the book I love the best "Enter the Sea Of Unlimited Consciousness" what a pure and simple way to describe the different levels that the soul must do to grow. To take a step into the depths of the soul to journey toward the light takes so much courage. Michele has that courage and wisdom that she explains here in her book. She holds your hand to feel safe as you step forward and dive into the sea. If you are ready to experience the depths of your own soul then this is a must read book. I highly recommend this book to anyone who wants to understand what they truly came here to do.
Carol Guy, Angelic Counselor

I am a young guy and I find this a very enlightening and entertaining book. It helps me to see in a cool way how we are so much more than our bodies and how I can use my mind to become all I could ever dream of and at the same time learn more about Spirit. **T. Rogers**

The book was well written and very easy reading. The method is so simple that you would never really consider it on your own. Michele Blood is a fabulous, beautiful and spiritual woman with much to share with the world. Her pairing up with Bob Proctor for this project is a gift for all of us.
Patricia Mulligan

This book has so much wisdom! Bob and Michele do an excellent job, teaching the spiritual laws to magnetize money through your service to others. More importantly, the book explains how to experience real wealth monetarily and spiritually. This book is for you if you truly want to be wealthy and learn to swim deeply in the sea of unlimited consciousness. Get this book for a comprehensive, yet easy-to-understand guide to dramatically attract money to you and increase your level of consciousness.
Mujiba Salaam Parker "Mujiba.com"

"Become A magnet To Money Through the Sea of Unlimited Consciousness" is an amazing book! It is written with clear awareness of the stages of our soul's growth, explained with such clarity, depth, knowledge, sensitivity, and fun! I will be reading it again and again to absorb and feel the fullness of its content. Michele Blood is a deeply spiritual, incredibly vivacious, infectious, spiritual leader. Her rare enthusiasm and soul sensitivity is such an inspiration. This rare explanation of the soul's growth gives us great insight as to where we are in our spiritual progression. "Become a Magnet to Money" gives you all the steps you need to achieve the success you desire. After much searching for the answers to attain success, I am at peace knowing all the information and the practical action steps I need to live the life of my dreams are in this book!! An added bonus is access to Michele Blood's uplifting singing. The combination of words created by Bob Proctor and Michele's enthusiastic talent stays with you daily to heal and uplift! This book has been written with such free-spirited joy and depth of knowledge, making it truly inspirational, practical, and deeply helpful to attain our dreams, and raise our spiritual awareness to much higher levels of FUN and deep inner PEACE. **Joan Marie (spiritual artist)**

This volume is amazing. This is the best book I have ever read describing so simply the levels of spiritual consciousness and done with such depth and humor. I literally could not put it down once I started reading. I recommend this book for any seeker on the path and also to someone who may not be sure if they are suffering from depression or as Michele says a dark night of the soul. I also recommend it to anyone in the medical field.
Kathleen Reinhardt, Psychiatric RN

Introduction to...
parts one and two

With this revised edition we have added a few more insights into truly understanding consciousness. We did this because of the many requests and questions we received via e-mails and letters. This touched our hearts deeply, for these individuals truly wish to have a deeper understanding. We thank you for your letters. Because you asked these questions this will then serve to allow others to understand as well. We are ALL deeply grateful for your voice. We have looked through these requests and added what we pray will give even greater clarity for all who read. It truly is simple but at the same time quite deep. That's God for you! And please always remember, it is also FUN! So keep your humour, clown nose and joy close by at all times.

Every book of true spiritual wisdom we have read has brought about some measure of higher awareness to our consciousness, what might be called the *melting down of ice* or *peeling of an onion* to who we really are. Each book, seminar, or spiritual experience has been taken into consciousness and has prepared us for the next spiritual realization. As we awaken more to the Truth of who we really are, we begin to live in two worlds: one of Light and one of the so called *real world.* This can be a challenge to an open heart. Those who have had a true spiritual awakening, discover coming back down to earth where bills have to be paid and business conducted to be very challenging and sometimes even painful.

May this book in two magical parts awaken the *greatness in you* so that you can experience this world and at the same time keep waking up more and more to your true spiritual self. Let these words help you prosper with an increase of money, power and Light. Feel it for your self, for there is far more going on in this volume than mere words. As you read, please keep your mind focused and your heart open and you *will* receive the message. You will know!

Many of you reading this material may have seen Bob Proctor for the first time in the now world renowned film "The Secret" and the film "Beyond The Secret". Both films are a great introduction to metaphysics, the laws that govern this universe and the films serve as a true reminder the *importance of consciousness*. These films and others that are now coming out are helping ignite the Divine Spark of Consciousness and can open a whole new world of new awareness and possibilities. For many, these films will be the first introduction to *Spiritual Universal Laws*. However, for the serious student of consciousness, the question is *what's next?* How do we use the universal laws to YES attract money, success but most importantly, how do we experience Oneness through *spiritual awareness*? Well, that is where this magical volume comes in, to answer what's next! Prosperity Consciousness goes much deeper than just thinking good thoughts and having a good attitude, even though mindfulness is of course very important if we wish to awaken to Truth!

Let me share with you first a little about Bob Proctor. Bob Proctor is, in my opinion, a true transformational prosperity teacher. He has high awareness, a beautiful heart and has the rare ability to teach people from all walks of life and cultures the secrets to success so that anyone can really understand and get IT! Bob's best selling book "You Were Born Rich" and his audio programs and live events have changed the lives of millions of souls all over the world. Bob is a true mentor to so many great authors and teachers of our time, he has helped people from all over the world to wake up and lead a life of prosperity.

I am deeply grateful that I met Bob Proctor and had the honor and privilege to work with him. He is a beautiful and wise soul. When I first started working with Bob in 1992 it changed my life. He asked me "*Michele, what do you truly want?*" No one had ever asked me that before. I thought about it and realized I wanted freedom and awareness so that I could spread more Light through my positive music and help as many people as I could on my journey. I had already done one album on my own as a solo artist. Without my band mates and being in a new country alone *it* was scary. Bob said to me "*So what if you're scared, do it scared, if it doesn't scare you a little then your want is not Big Enough.*" WOW those words changed my thinking about fear. It was GOOD to be scared as then I was growing. What a concept. Because of Bob's amazing light and wisdom our MusiVation™ music is now spreading Light all over the world.

Bob's friendship and guidance was such a blessing in my life and helped me in so many ways. He began writing songs with me as he really understood how powerful and fast positive affirmations created as lyrics would be to the mind when combined with melody and music. Together we created such powerful MusiVation™ songs and then we went on to create the most beautiful and powerful audio programs on Success. I still have pages of lyrics Bob has written that are filled with light and wisdom. I will continue writing music for his words/lyrics because they are overflowing with such a HIGH VIBRATION of wisdom, power and light. That is why people feel so high after listening to the songs as the light behind the recordings is HIGH! As Bob says "*Vibration tells the story every time.*"

Part One in this volume **"Become A Magnet To Money"** holds many Universal Truths with clear instructions, so that all who are ready to take action on these ideas and follow the instructions will be inspired, and can be very successful and happy. I took transcripts from audio programs I recorded with Bob many years ago and put what I consider the greatest of his lessons from these MusiVation™ programs into Part One and then wrote and added more topics. Many people *do* still prefer the written word and in a book form the teachings can then follow on through the years and help many more souls, long after we have left our physical bodies. (We also have a powerful version of this book as an audio book.)

As Doug Wead, former Special Assistant to the President of the United States stated about Bob Proctor *"Zig Ziglar may be the master motivator, Mark Victor Hansen and Jack Canfield of Chicken Soup for the Soul, the master story tellers; Anthony Robins may be the guru of personal development, but Bob Proctor is The Master Thinker. No one can touch him."* The Master Thinker wow!! Doug Wead is an aware soul; he really gets who Bob is!

Part Two, **"The Sea Of Unlimited Consciousness"** originally started out as the last chapter Part One and then Spirit had more plans for this topic and guided me to go into more depth of discussion into *why* we experience certain confusion and doubts through the different levels of consciousness. The 2nd part of this book gives some guidance to all you may be feeling as you rise higher into oneness of Divine consciousness. For example what is a *dark night of the soul* compared to *depression*? Most do not realize that a *dark night of the soul* experience is actually a good thing because no one explained to them what they were experiencing. Some did in fact go backwards instead of moving forward. Usually at these times we go to a therapist to find out what is wrong but it is only through esoteric illumination and meditative contemplation we can know for sure, no one can know for us. We can however be guided so that we can understand what we are experiencing and not think we are sometimes perhaps going a little crazy.

What has this to do with wealth and success? Well everything. Why we get stuck at some stages of our development is discussed in Part Two. Part One is more instructional. So if you have been on the path and feel that your spiritual studies and practices are no longer working Part Two in this magical volume may illuminate you, which is the intention. That is why there are Two Parts in one volume. It is recommended that you read Part One "Become A Magnet To Money" first and then read Part Two **"The Sea Of Unlimited Consciousness"** second.

So many Enlightened minds and souls have been teaching these truths about the power of our thoughts and meditation and mysticism for eons of time from Augustas (Hermes) Trismigestus, The Buddha, Jesus the Christ and all of the great authors of positive thinking of the past 100 years, Norman Vincent Peale, Napoleon Hill, Joel S Goldsmith, Wallace D. Wattles etc. all these great minds said basically the same thing in different ways, *"Thoughts are Things, As Above So Below, With Your Thoughts You Create The World, Only Thinking Makes It So, It Is Your Faith etc"* A Master Thinker is one who knows and feels intensely their connection to their higher power. Bob is a Master Thinker and has brought the *Law of Attraction* and *how to think* to the masses from all cultures and to people from all walks of life and even into the hard nosed corporate world. As of this date in 2009 he has done this for over 40 years and he is still going strong.

This volume holds words of Truth. Powerful lessons to help you become a wealthy, independent *free* soul. So if this is new to you please keep an open mind and let your heart *feel* it for you. May you always walk consciously with Spirit and may your life be increased with abundance, joy and illumination. Always remember that Life Is Magical...

Wealth and Happiness

"Before I had a lot of money, I was really quite happy. And I'll tell you this, you may not believe it, I never would have gotten the money if I wasn't happy to begin with. I never would have gotten it."

Oprah Winfrey said that and Oprah has a lot of money. Money that she earned. Yes, Oprah knows something about attracting money. She also has a lot of friends and literally millions of admirers all over the world. You would be safe in saying that Oprah Winfrey is truly a rich woman. I feel she is also a very wealthy woman. Wealth is enjoying what we have. We are wealthy when we love ourselves for what we are and not what we have. I believe that describes Oprah Winfrey. I want to suggest that we begin by thanking God for the many marvelous faculties with which you and I have been blessed.

Let's begin by being happy and grateful!

Henry Ward Beacher pointed out that wealth is not an end of life, but an instrument of life. The following information contains specific instructions on how you can magnetize yourself to money. That's right, you will. Which is precisely why this carries the title, "Become A Magnet To Money." Listen to the MusiVation™ song every day we have gifted you.

Keep singing the song, listen to it every day *"Money, Money loves me. I Am a Magnet To Money."*

Hello, this is Bob Proctor and I'm having a great time because once again I've teamed up with that international singing sensation, Michele. Together we're bringing you paradigm altering lessons and information.

As you have already discovered, this book deals with one of my favorite subjects, *money*. To become the magnet Michele is singing about there are a few beautiful truths you must first consciously consider. You must then properly plant these truths in the treasury of your subconscious mind. When you have accomplished that, you will feel the money magnetism which you already posses. This book is especially designed to assist you in successfully completing the process which creates the magnetism you are seeking.

I've often thought it to be rather strange, and I should probably add sad, that earning money is not taught in our school systems anywhere in the world. The frequent response to this kind of thinking is, "*Why should we teach money as a subject in school, everyone already understands how to earn money?*" However, that is not correct. The sad truth is that 97 out of every 100 people live and die without ever developing any real expertise in this area. They never learn the most basic steps of earning money. As a result most people live from payday to payday. To perpetuate this ridiculous problem their ignorance is passed along from one generation to the next. Conversely, the 3-4% of our population who *do* understand how to attract wealth pass their prosperity consciousness from one generation to the next. The rich get rich, and the poor get, well, not much.

To properly understand how you can magnetize yourself to money, *first* you must have an open mind, *second,* you must remain objective, and *third,* you must understand that the universe operates in an exact way which many people refer to as natural law. I prefer to refer to these laws as Divine Laws. They are God's Modus Operandi, nothing happens by accident. You are not reading this information by accident you are ready to learn and accept these great Universal Divine Laws.

One of the basic laws is the law that states, *"Everything is moving. Absolutely nothing rests."* You are either moving ahead in life, or you are going backwards.

Grow or die. Create or disintegrate.

You are becoming richer or poorer.

There's another important law which is referred to in many different ways: Karmic law, Sowing and Reaping, Law of Attraction, Cause and Effect, Action/Reaction. How you refer to this law is of little importance, but the understanding of how it works is vitally important.

The thoughts, feelings, and actions that you express in life are the seeds that you sow. The conditions, circumstances, and things that come into your life are the harvest you reap as a result of the seeds you sow.

The apostle Matthew stated, *"To him who has much shall be given, and he shall have abundance. But from him who does not have, even that which he has shall be taken away."* At first glance that sure doesn't sound very fair. Matthew is saying that the rich get richer and the poor, poorer. People who believe this as unfair are people who view abundance as something that is being doled out. To them Matthew's statement will have to appear grossly unfair. If, however, you see abundance as something one attracts the entire picture would change and it would be very fair. The prosperous person will be thinking prosperous thoughts and attracting more of the same. While the poor person will be thinking of lack and limitation and, by law, will attract more of the same.

Abundance is something we magnetize ourselves to. Business associates, opportunities, sales, money, love, friends, everything we want will come into our life by law not luck. You are either attracting or repelling good. It is your own consciousness that ultimately determines your results.

It is time for the 97% group to
Wake up!

Almost everyone can learn how to make money. It's equally important to understand that there's no limit with respect to how much money you can earn. Very few people know or believe what I just said. That is precisely why there are so many poor, old people. This book and the MusiVation™ mind music is their wake up call.

There have been many excellent books written over the years which tell you how to earn money. I personally consider Napoleon Hill's book, *"Think and Grow Rich,"* to be one of the most complete works ever compiled on the accumulation of wealth. In the publisher's preface of the book it is stated that *"Think and Grow Rich", conveys the experience of more than 500 individuals of great wealth who began from scratch with nothing to give in return for riches except thoughts, ideas, and organized plans.* It clearly states that this book contains the entire philosophy of money making.

The point I want to bring to your attention is this, *"Think and Grow Rich"* has 15 chapters and not one of those chapters is titled "Money". In fact even the word is not even in any one of the chapters. The last chapter has eight words in it, but money is not one of them.

Another great book about money was written by G. Donald Walters titled, *"Money Magnetism."* Mr. Walters has fourteen chapters in his book and not one is titled *"Money."* The word does appear in the title of chapter nine. Listen to how it is used, *"How Earning Money Can Promote Spiritual Growth."* Robert Russell's great book about earning money, *"You Too Can Be Prosperous,"* contains eight chapters and money is not anywhere in any of the eight titles.

Why do you suppose none of these books talk about money, when the purpose of the book is to assist the reader in accumulating wealth? They do not talk about money for the same reason a farmer does not take time explaining how to bring the harvest in when he is teaching his son how to plant a field. There's a season for sowing, and there's a season for reaping, but you never do both in the same season.

If you purchased this volume looking for an inside tip for the stock market, which mutual fund might yield the highest rate of interest, or any other subject of that nature which deals with money, you will probably be miserably disappointed. However if you have a sincere desire to attract increasing amounts of money from multiple sources on a continual basis, money which will enable you to do greater good for yourself and others, you've made a wise investment.

YOUR FREE MONEY SONG

We have included an MP3 of the powerful MusiVation ™ song
I Am A Magnet To Money!
Do not underestimate the power that comes to you when these lyrics enter your subconscious. Simply type the link below into your Internet Browser to receive the song. It is an important part of the lessons you will receive in this book. You will be given instructions on how to use the MusiVation™ mind technology throughout the book.
www.MysticalSuccessClub.com/MoneySong

Prosperity Consciousness
"An ideal is an idea you have fallen in Love with!"
James Allen

Give serious thought to what I'm about to say. The paper you fold and place in your purse or your pocket *is not money*. It is paper with ink on it. It represents money, but it is not money.

Money is an *idea.*

All over the world paper money is quickly being replaced with plastic cards and with the technological changes that are rapidly taking place, it would appear that the life of the credit card is not going to be very long. Your earning of money has nothing to do with paper or plastic, it has to do with *consciousness.* That is precisely why all of these great authors I spoke of in the first chapter wrote books, books which people claim helped them earn millions of dollars, never wrote specifically about money. They were instructional manuals on how to develop *prosperity consciousness,* which in turn will magnetize you to money.

I wrote a book about money titled, *"You Were Born Rich,"* and you were. Rich in potential. "You Were Born Rich" is sold worldwide in a number of languages. Like this book, "Born Rich" deals with the cause of wealth. Many millionaires on the opposite sides of the globe credit the information from the book, "You Were Born Rich," with changing their life. You will soon be giving this exciting book along with our MusiVation™ songs, credit for your great wealth.

I am aware there are books which instruct you on how to manipulate market stocks and people; they might even help you get money. But there's no spiritual strength there, and if there's no spiritual strength there's no lasting happiness, no real wealth.

Many years ago I sat and listened intently as W. Clement Stone explained to me how he had sat up all night reading Loyd C. Douglas' masterpiece, *"The Magnificent Obsession,"* and then went on to earn his great fortune. Loyd C. Douglas' book is not about earning money. The basic premise that entire book is built on is *giving.* If you want money, ask for abundance in all areas of your life then study, understand, and follow the laws for sowing which will insure an abundant harvest in all areas of your life.

If you want to solve a problem you must first attack the *cause* of the problem. The cause of poverty is poverty consciousness. Poverty consciousness causes a person to see, hear, think, smell, and feel lack and limitation. When wealthy people experience a financial problem in their life, which is not uncommon, they possess the wisdom to focus on the cause of the problem. They make the mental corrections required and proceed. Listen to the conversations of individuals with poverty consciousness. Lack, limitation, and tough times are all they talk about. That is all they talk about because that is all they think about. That's all they think about because they have a poverty consciousness and they permit their present results to control their thinking.

Pay particular attention to what I am about to explain...Permitting *present results* to control ones thoughts and actions is the most common of all errors made insofar as human development is concerned. You have very likely been programmed all of your life to do that. What does the school report card do? Graduate that through multiple examples through sales reports, to hospital x-rays, to your bank statement.

Present results are the manifestation of past thinking.

Focusing on present results will cause a strain of conscious thought which are a replica of your past thoughts.

Really take these truths in!! Are you beginning to see why the vast majority of people keep getting the same type of results year after year? They keep going to the same movie, over and over again, people must learn to stop pressing the same buttons...

Stop Pressing The Same Buttons

I heard a woman speaking on television about herself and an associate getting on an elevator. They had been deeply involved in a conversation when the elevator doors opened. They got on the elevator while they continued with their conversation. They said after a few moments the elevator doors had closed but they were not going anywhere. She continued explaining that they had either pressed the button for the floor they were on or they had not pressed a button at all. I could relate to her story because I have done the same thing on occasion and I would imagine you have probably done the same thing as well. The woman who was speaking went on to explain that was how most people lived their lives. They keep pressing the same buttons. They focus on what they've got instead of what they want.

Don't attempt to earn or attract the amount of money you *think* you can earn. Decide how much you want and then discipline yourself to think the way you have to think to attract what you want.

The famous movie maker, the late Mike Todd, once stated, *"Being broke is a temporary situation. Being poor is a mental state."* He was correct. There are wealthy people who lose every cent they have through a series of mistakes in judgment. That does not make them poor. They will get their money back in a short time because of their prosperity consciousness. They know which buttons they have to push. Study the research that has been done on poor people who win lotteries. In a short time they have nothing left. Money cannot stay with a person who has a poverty consciousness. The flip side of the coin is also true. Money cannot stay away from the person who possesses a prosperity consciousness. *The wealthy person has a prosperity consciousness.*

They understand there is an Infinite Source of supply.

They are acutely aware of the fact that if they are experiencing a problem with the harvest, if there is not sufficient or more than sufficient harvest to meet all of their needs, they are the cause of the problem. Perhaps they have not properly prepared the land, sown sufficient seeds, or sown seeds in enough fields. They loathe lack and limitation. They demand the abundant, the good life which is their birthright.

And when they experience any less they take full and complete responsibility for their possession. Blame is not part of their way of life. They will not talk about lack because their prosperity consciousness will not permit it. They know they must press the button representing the floor they want. They know that talking about lack is sowing seeds for more of the same. They immediately begin to brainstorm with other individuals who have a prosperity consciousness about other crops they want to harvest in the future and where they should begin sowing. That is what these lessons are going to inspire you to do as well.

Multiple Sources of Income
(MSI's)

How much money do you want? It is your choice. There is only now, so choose now how much you really want?

If you have any question in your mind regarding where your consciousness is, it is not difficult to find out. Be very honest with yourself and look at your results. Study the patterns in your life. How much money do you want? Saying, *"I want more,"* is not good enough. Five dollars more is more.

How much more?

You must be specific. You should have the amount of money you need and desire to provide the things you want, the way *you* choose to live. You will not seriously want more money than you are capable of earning, but remember you must earn it and there are only two ways to earn money!

1) Money at Work   2) People at Work

Remember that. One is money at work and the second is people at work. You must be employing both. If you want to be financially independent what you are actually saying is this, *"I want to have more than enough money working for me to provide the income I require to live the way I choose to live."*

What you have just read may cause you to think that you'll have to quit your present job because you cannot see yourself earning the amount of money that you require in your present position. Although that may be true, it does not have to be true.

Work is made for you;
you are not made for work.

Most of your pleasures in life come from your labor not your leisure. The amount of money you earn from your daily work is not, let me repeat, is not the most important consideration. The most important consideration about your daily work is that you love what you do. Let me repeat that...

The most important consideration about your daily work is that *you LOVE what you do.*

It's not uncommon for people who earn very high annual incomes to receive just a small percent of their annual income from their daily work. Many political positions are filled by individuals who receive one dollar a year. Where do you think their income is coming from?

With few exceptions, people with high annual incomes all have MSI's!

Multiple Sources of Income.

Multiple sources of income and multiple jobs are quite different. At one point in my life I did not understand the difference. I had five jobs at one time. I would go from one to the other. I thought I was on the right road to financial freedom. I was actually on the road to an early death. Fortunately I became aware of the difference between a job and a source of income before it was too late.

Now this is another point I want to repeat because it's very important to your happiness and your health.

Multiple sources of income,
does not mean multiple jobs.

The individuals who live the most fulfilled lives are those who have a very difficult time differentiating between work and pleasure. That's a key factor in living the abundant life. I only have one job. I only have one job and I love it. When you love what you do you will never have to work again. MSI's will frequently, although not always, be closely associated with your work since that would be your area of expertise.

Permit me to draw on my own personal experience in an effort to clarify the concept of multiple sources of income. My personal area of expertise is assisting individuals in altering paradigms, their mental conditioning, which permits these individuals to effectively adapt to change and improve the results they are getting in their life. My daily work: I write and conduct seminars for small, medium, and major corporations worldwide. In the seminars I assist the employees of these corporations to alter their old paradigms which help the employee improve the quality of their life. These seminars also make the employees more valuable to the company.

Now my multiple sources of income: I'll name a few. I have audio and DVD/Video educational programs being marketed by other people in various countries. I have books in various languages being sold in many countries. My educational programs are advertised and sold in magazines and on the Internet and bookstores. I'm extremely fortunate in that I write lyrics for the MusiVation™ songs which are produced and recorded by Michele, who is the international singing star of positive mind changing MusiVation™ music. One such CD is titled, **"Songs for SUCCESS,"** and another is "Songs for MotiVation," and these CD's are sold in book and music stores, Amazon.com and other sites internationally.

I have fun creating and love all of my many MSI's. When establishing MSI's I want to suggest that you too make them fun. Make them interesting and make them profitable. You can have as many sources of income as you can imagine or want.

Network Marketing is one of the most powerful and fastest growing concepts in the world today. It has made many millionaires. Individuals who are members of a network marketing company have multiple sources of income. They could conceivably have thousands of them. Network marketing is one of the very best ways of establishing multiple sources of income. If you are not already involved in a network marketing company give it consideration. Make sure you pick a good one. Investigate the owners of the company and make sure that they are operating with sound business principles and then they must have an excellent product line.

Fall in love with the products. If you love a movie you tell all your friends to go watch it, in a network marketing company you are simply doing the same thing, sharing with people information about a product you love but this way you get paid for letting people know about products that you use and love.

On the next page we have an example of what Bob created for an MSI mind map. Of course this is to not to scale. Create a much larger one for your office space or home.

Multiple Sources of Income (MSIs) is one of the ways the rich get richer. Now you too can learn...

How Money and Success Come to You!

In the spaces provided, fill in 2 (or more) added sources of income that you will develop. A Primary Source of Income (PSI) is where you must be present. An MSI is where money is being made without your being present.

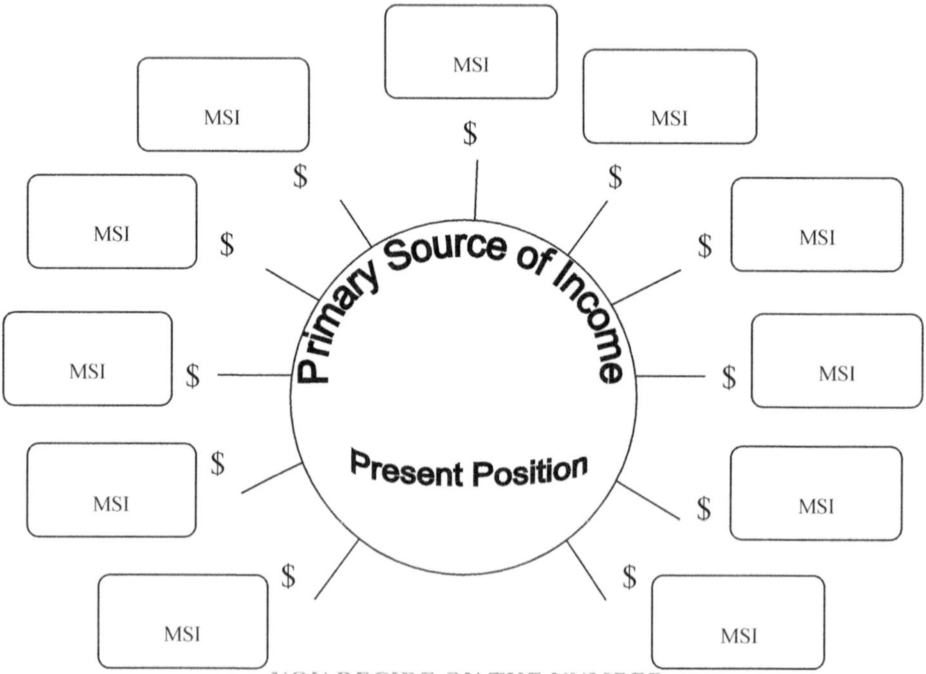

YOU DECIDE ON THE NUMBER OF MSI's YOU WILL HAVE

Designed by
Bob Proctor

Providing Service

Money is a reward received for service rendered.

When you understand this basic law you will understand the only time you must think about money is when you are deciding how much you want. From that point on your entire focus intellectually, emotionally, physically, must be directed towards *providing service.*

You and I were put on the planet to serve one another. Thinking of ways we can be of greater service will enable us to grow *intellectually and spiritually.*

Money is the ultimate servant.

With money you can provide service in a thousand places at the same time. The more money you earn the more you can help others. The more you help others the more money you will earn...

A beautiful prosperity cycle.

It's your own personal wheel of fortune. Think of how you can do whatever you are doing more effectively. Think about how you can improve on the quality and the quantity of the service you are rendering. Think of how you can help the people you are helping in a greater way.

It's very important for you to keep money in the proper place in your mind. Money will not make you a better person, *but it can make you more effective.* Money will not make you happy although it will make you more comfortable. And always remember this; money will not make you smarter.

In the movie, "*Born Yesterday*" staring Melanie Griffith and John Goodman. Melanie Griffith took on the character Billie Dawn. Her script had her appear as a dumb, blonde bimbo most of the way through the movie when in truth Billie was far from being dumb. John Goodman played Harry Braun who is a somewhat drunken, wealthy, wheeler-dealer business man. Harry thought everyone had a price. That he could buy anything and anyone with money. He was always talking about how much money he had. Near the end of the movie the tables were turned, Billie accused Harry of being dumb. Harry responded to Billie saying, *"Do you think a person with this much money is dumb?"* Billie proved to be anything but dumb when she answered, *"I don't think you're dumb, Harry. I know you're dumb. Only a dumb person would think money would make them smart."* Melanie Griffith's character nailed it. Only a dumb person would think money would do anything for them beyond the possibility of making them more effective or more comfortable.

Let's look at it this way. Since money will make you more effective and will definitely make you more comfortable, you might as well have all you want. Personally I want an ever increasing amount of money coming to me on a constant basis through multiple sources. I want to be more effective and I definitely want to be more comfortable. And I'm proceeding on the premise that you do as well.

There's another important point of money that I want to share with you that I picked up watching a video that was sent to me by my good friend Jane Willhite. Jane is the chairperson of PSI World seminars. A very powerful lady. It was a tape of a speech made by William Pen Patrick in 1972. What an incredible speech. It's called, *"First Day, Last Day."* And I want to say that this is one of the best speeches I've ever heard, and believe me I've heard a few.

Pen Patrick said, *"You will hear people saying money is sinful or evil but money cannot be sinful or evil. Money does not have a mind or a soul therefore it cannot be immoral or unethical. Some people who have a lot of money are sinful or evil, but there are many poor people who are just as sinful and evil."*

There are people literally held in poverty because they do not understand what William Pen Patrick said. They have been raised with the idea they should not want money. As children, whenever the subject of money was raised, they were given great doses of A-1, Grade-A, High quality, First class GUILT. That was because the people raising these children had no money and they didn't want the children asking for money. If that happened to you permit me to suggest that you forgive the idea immediately. Mentally release the idea that money is evil or sinful. That's what *forgive* means, to let go of completely, release it, abandon it, and immediately replace the old idea with the new idea: money is an excellent servant. Ask the universe for money, all you want. Ask believing you will receive, and bingo you're magnetized.

An Infinite Supply

Money is in the ether. Oh yes it is. An infinite supply, yes, yes. I love it. You may remember a quote by Henry Ward Beacher where he referred to money, *as an instrument of light.* I previously pointed out that the only time you should think about money itself is when you are deciding how much you want. Well, I'm going to share a couple of beautiful ideas that you can use when you're deciding how much you want.

Begin by dreaming of all the good things that you want to do and the fun, joyful experiences you want. Write it all down and do not limit yourself, not even for a second. Keep reminding yourself *the cost of what you want is unimportant* because you receive your supply from an *Infinite Source.* When you get the picture of what you want, it may cost a few thousand, a few hundred thousand, or a million. That doesn't really matter. Henry Ford once suggested if you take a big job and break it into small parts you'll make it easy. So let's pick a big number. Let's make it easy.

I've already discussed the merits of multiple sources of income, well this is where you decide how many sources you begin to establish. You might state, *"Twenty four months from today I will have five sources of income."* Make it ten or twenty if you want, there are no limits. You pick the number then divide the gross figure you want to earn by the number of MSI's you have decided to establish. The big figure will very quickly shrink.

Build yourself an income visualization chart!
(as shown earlier)

First...get a piece of art board and in the center draw a circle about 1 ½ inches in diameter. Write in that circle, PSI. Which stands for Primary Source Of Income.

Second...about 6 inches out from your PSI circle make a series of smaller circles all the way around it about ¾ of an inch in diameter. The smaller circles will be your MSI's.

This visualization chart is going to look like a big wheel with your primary source of income as the hub. All the smaller sources of income around it will represent your multiple sources of income. Your multiple sources of income as I've stated over and over again is where you choose how many you are going to create. It's not important to know what each MSI will be when you determine the number. Always remember that nature abhors a vacuum. You've created a space for the amount of money you desire when you make your income visualization chart.

The chart will cause you to think of sources of income to fill those spaces. An age old adage says, *"Seek and you will find"* and this is accurate. Never neglect your responsibility to your primary source of income. You should forever be attempting to execute your duties at your primary source of income in a more professional manner. Follow that advice as if it were a sacred law. The more professional you become the more your reputation will grow until you become an acknowledged expert in your field. It will soon be apparent the more your status grows, the more expertise you develop in your primary source of income, the more opportunities for multiple sources of income will come your way. You will become a magnet to money. That is when you will truly understand what Michele is singing about.

The Law of Relativity
&
Income Acceleration

Now comes a beautiful idea I want to share with you. It is a powerhouse.

When arriving at the amount of money you want to earn. Work in harmony with the *Law of Relativity.* Follow along with me. If a person is presently earning let's say $35,000 a year, and they're doing what the masses do, they will begin to ask themselves if they can earn $45,000 a year and then possibly $50,000 maybe $60,000. They might even work they're way up to $75,000. Wherever they stop the number will look big. *I mean really big*. It will seem like a lot of money because they will be relating it to what they are presently earning. That is using the *Law of Relativity* against themselves. Poor people do this all of the time.

Now, let's take a look at the flip side of the coin.

What do the high income earners do?

Well, let's think about this. You're working with an Infinite Source of supply, you have a marvelous mind, and all things are possible. Napoleon Hill nailed it when he said, *"Anything the mind can conceive and believe it can achieve."* Forget the past. Ignore your present results. Dream. Let your mind soar...

Get a pen and a pad, get a calculator, and play the game I love to play. Do this now! Remember there is only NOW.

Choose what appears to be a ridiculously high figure. I'm going to use an example of let's say five million dollars. Write that figure at the top of a sheet of paper.

Now your objective is to seriously think of how you will earn that amount of money in a twelve month period of time. Keep the MSI concept working for you. You might have difficulty solving this challenge. Then again you might not. One thing is certain, you will never solve it if you don't take action. That's the very reason so few people have that kind of money. They never think of how they could. Well you too can play this game and be different. Turn this exercise into enjoyable experience. An enjoyable pastime. I invest an enormous amount of time doing exercises of this nature.

Find a very comfortable environment. You might choose the most exclusive hotel in your area. Find a quiet corner in the lounge. Get a sandwich and a cup of tea or coffee and stay there for two or three hours by yourself *and think.* How can I do this? How can I earn five million dollars in one year?

Have your calculator, your pen and pad ready. Break it into small parts. You'll begin to solve this self created puzzle a bit at a time. Turn this exercise into a ritual. Go to your chosen opulent environment say every Tuesday afternoon or every Thursday morning. Make certain no one knows where you are going. And make certain no one knows what you are doing. There must be no disturbances. Don't even tell anyone what you're doing. This is your *income acceleration* thinking time. Don't become chatty with the person who is serving you. Become invisible. Dress well but not in anything that will make you stand out, no bright colors. You might even develop a reputation of a person with little or no social intelligence wherever you happen to be while mentally playing this little game.

For the first few weeks that you're involved in this exercise you may produce nothing that you can see but you ARE creating in mind and you will reap rewards so keep at it. This is a new talent you're working on. Stay with it and you'll become very proficient at earning money. I have. Many of my friends have and so will you.

Now after you have played with the five million figure for a while take a break. And if you're having real trouble lower the number. Drop down to four million or maybe three million. Keep doing that but understand this, where ever you stop, the number will seem small relative to the five million you started with. This is getting you IN TUNE with money. You are now gaining *Prosperity Consciousness.* Now that's how to work in harmony with the *Law of Relativity.* And to become a magnet to money, you have to work in harmony with all the laws of the Universe including the *Law of Relativity.*

It takes approximately fifty hours flying time to travel right around the world. One year I traveled to Malaysia every single month. If you look at a map of the world you're going to find that from Toronto, Malaysia is on the other side of the world. That meant I had to go around the world every month. Needless to say that's a lot of time in the air. Now I fly First Class, and that by the way is how you should travel. In fact that's how you should live. The world will never treat you better than the way you treat yourself. I mention this because I want you to know that I'm extremely well taken care of during my fifty hours in the air.

The game I explained should be taken very seriously. I have on occasion been playing this game I'm referring to for the entire fifty hours I'm in the air, flying to and from Malaysia to Toronto. This game is like a puzzle. You create a puzzle and then you focus all of your mental energy on solving the puzzle. It's important that you are comfortable. It's vitally important that you're in a comfortable environment while you're creating the solution to your financial puzzle. I know I've mentioned that before, but it is very, very important. So go ahead and play this powerful game and let The Law of Relativity and action accelerate your income.

Renew Your Marvelous Mind

Now with all that has been said in previous chapters lets get down to the how? How do you renew your marvelous mind so that you are in perfect harmony with the amount of money you want; so you are magnetized to money?

Let's start here by you saying this powerful affirmation. I am a magnet to money. Come on you say it with me. I am a magnet to money. Listen to Michele singing; go back to the MP3 of this MusiVation™ song we gifted you with this book...

**I AM A MAGNET TO MONEY
I NOW HAVE MORE
THAN I NEED
I AM A MAGNET TO MONEY
$$ MONEY, MONEY LOVES ME**

Now I want you to turn the sound up and sing along with Michele. That's right you've got to sing along with her. Don't worry about what you sound like. If you have ever heard me sing you would understand that it doesn't matter what you sound like!

**I AM A MAGNET TO MONEY
I NOW HAVE MORE
THAN I NEED
I AM A MAGNET TO MONEY
$$ MONEY, MONEY LOVES ME**

Just wait until you see what listening to and singing along to this powerful affirmation mind renewing MusiVation™ song is doing for you. In fact let's examine what's happening when you're singing along or even when you're simply listening to Michele.

A transformation in your subconscious mind is beginning to take place. It probably wasn't noticeable. In fact you'd have a very difficult time measuring it. Never the less your subconscious mind was being transformed. That is what MusiVation™ is all about. The music, the melody and the instrumental, affects the right hemisphere of your brain, then when you sing and think about the lyrics the left hemisphere of your brain is also affected. This approach is called MusiVation™. It stimulates the whole brain. Both the right and left hemispheres of the brain. MusiVation™ has proved to be a fast and highly effective approach to altering a person's subconscious conditioning which in turn changes their life.

Now, you think in pictures. And through constant spaced repetition you impress the picture concept the lyrics represent upon the subconscious mind.

What I am about to say is extremely important....

Your subconscious conditioning or your paradigm will determine your logic.

What I'm going to be asking you to do may very likely appear to be totally illogical relative to your present paradigm. However great improvements frequently if not always call for an almost total disregard to logic.

Really take in these words carefully. In 1899 Charles H. Duell said, *"Everything that can be invented, has been invented."* He was the director of the United States Patent Office that year. Moving ahead, Robert Milligan in 1923 said, *"There is not likelihood that man can ever tap the power of the atom."* He won the Nobel Prize that year for physics.

Here's another beauty, in 1905 Grover Cleveland said, "*Sensible and responsible women do not want to vote."* Can you even imagine a United States president saying anything like that today? All of that was logical in the mind of the masses back around the turn of the previous century. It is sheer nonsense today, but it wasn't nonsense over a hundred years ago.

Breakthroughs are made from violating logic!

I want you to violate your logic. If you want to develop *prosperity consciousness* you must renew you mind. You must do what many consider to be totally illogical. That takes something special, and you have that something special or you wouldn't have been attracted to this book.

J. Paul Getty was one of the richest people who ever lived. Personally I have received many valuable tips from his writings. Getty pointed out that all a person would need to make the transformation I am suggesting, is an independent mind and an ounce of courage. You've got that. The good life is not difficult, but it sure is different. You are going to be amazed at how simple it is to make the transformation we are discussing. But remember the idea of magnetizing yourself to money is considered absolute insanity to the mind of the general population. That is why I previously emphasized the importance of the idea that our conditioned mind determines our logic. It is the conditioned mind of the general population which causes them to feel that it is a form of insanity to think that you can magnetize yourself to money. *You must not let that stop you!*

Now I'm going to paint a picture for you that will hopefully help you see this concept as I see it. I want this to make sense to you.

Permit the image of a swimming pool, an Olympic sized swimming pool to flow onto the screen of your mind. Close your eyes and let the image of a large swimming pool fill your consciousness. In your mind see yourself standing beside the pool in your bathing suit. You are standing on white tile which is all around the edge of the pool. The water in the pool is very dark blue in color. Someone has obviously polluted the water with some kind of dye coloring. You most certainly will not go in for a swim today. As you stand there a maintenance man walks over to explain what is happening.

This is what you would hear *"I'm sorry you are not able to go swimming today. We are cleaning the pool. Someone has dumped coloring into the pool overnight. The pool will probably be closed for a while. We have been working on the problem all day, although no one can see the result of our efforts yet. It is quite possible you will not see any visible change in the color of the water for a few days, however please understand something is being done. The pool has an excellent filtering system. There is clean, clear unpolluted water being pumped into the pool all day, and at the same time, the polluted water is being drained from the pool. It is a slow process but it is very effective. The clean, clear water is weakening the colored water, but because it is happening slowly you are not able to detect the difference with your eye. But you know if we just continue pumping clear, clean, unpolluted water in and continually drain the polluted water, in time the pool will become as clean and fresh as it once was, ready for swimming again."*

Believe me when I tell you this, your marvelous mind was once clean and clear. Pure unlimited power and prosperous high consciousness existed in your mind. Somehow your subconscious mind has been polluted with limiting, negative poverty concepts. How the pollution got there is irrelevant. I could explain it and you would understand, however these lessons are for you to understand the quickest and surest way to magnetize yourself to money.

Your subconscious mind is much like the pool. You'll not see a visible change in a hurry however know that if you continually pump in clean, pure, powerful, prosperity concepts the old conditioning will be weakened. Ultimately the truth will fill your consciousness, your mind will return to its pure, prosperous state. Evidence of this will appear in the physical world, yes *you will* see results. Yes, you will most certainly be openly rewarded for your faith. Believe, proceed, and succeed...

To make certain that you move into the vibration that is in complete harmony with the abundant life there are four concepts in which you have to give high priority. These four concepts must be firmly fixed in your subconscious mind. When that happens, doing what I'm about to suggest will be effortless because it will be a habit.

One You must begin every day with love in your heart and the attitude that your life has a new start.

Two Clearly understand there is always enough time to do what must be done. You must develop the proper perspective of time. You know that if you want something done you should give it to the person that's busy. They make time, literally. You will be that person. Yes you will. Michele is going to help you become that person with our MusiVation™ songs.

Three You will always have all the energy you need to do anything you'll ever want to do. No one gets energy. All the energy that ever was and forever will be is evenly present in all places at the same time. You are energy. You release energy. Desire is the triggering mechanism to release energy. You will become highly charged with energy when you and Michele begin singing about energy.

Four There is a law of vibration in the universe. Everything vibrates. The vibration you are in controls your actions and it also controls what you are attracting into your life, what you are magnetized to. You only attract that which is in harmony with you.

With all of these attitudes firmly fixed in your subconscious mind you will move into the vibration which causes you to do great work and for you to attract great rewards. *You will literally become a magnet to money.* You will always attract more than you need just like the powerful MusiVation™ lyrics say. Since love is harmony, or resonance, and you are in harmony with money, money will love you. It will flow freely to you and it will be your obedient servant.

You will do well to remember the advice of Lord Bacon he gave to his son. He said, *"Money is a good servant, but a bad master."* As Michele sings, let money serve you. It's such a pleasure working with Michele. She's such a professional, and she's so multi-talented. By doing what you are instructed to do you will transform your life. Read this over and over again and listen to the Magnet To Money song over and over again. Get all the MusiVation™ CD's, all of the songs have power lines and healthy attitudes. Michele sings each line over and over again because...

Repetition is the first law of learning.

Through the repetition of reading this over and over again and hearing and singing along with Michele these lessons will become firmly fixed in your subconscious mind. That is when they'll become a part of your way of thinking, a part of your way of life. That is when exciting and marvelous things will begin to happen in your life with constant regularity.

Permit me to caution you at this point. Understanding and acting on what I am about to say could conceivably be worth millions of dollars to you...

Your old paradigm which is your old conditioning is going to attempt to prevent you from playing the Magnet To Money and other MusiVation™ songs. The old conditioning your subconscious mind is in harmony with and the people you are surrounded by may try and stop you from using Michele's singing affirmations properly. I have already mentioned that your conditioned mind determines your logic. When your friends, relatives, and neighbors become aware of what you are doing they may laugh at you. They may tell you you're crazy. They may begin to talk about you to others. Your conscious mind will begin to think this doesn't make sense, this is totally illogical. You'll find yourself saying to yourself, *"I'm getting tired of listening to these songs over and over again."* It may possibly even begin to aggravate you. If, or when, all this happens rejoice and know that you are on the right road to a prosperous future.

Also do NOT tell your friends what you are doing if you fear they will mock you. Let your results speak for you. As Napoleon Hill said in his book 'Think and Grow Rich' *"Tell the world what you are going to do by first showing them."*

Let us now go back to the analogy of the pool with the dark blue polluted water. Let the image of the polluted pool represent your polluted conditioning. Conditioning that has kept you working hard for what is probably very little money. Take a look at most of the people you know. The people who will suggest listening to Michele and singing along with her everyday is silly. Where are those people financially? Most of those that mock you are probably losing. Understand that their subconscious mind is probably polluted as well.

Come with me mentally back to the pool. The pool of your conditioned, subconscious mind. Let this book and the songs along with your feeling/emotional involvement represent clean, clear water.

I'm sure that you now see that by impressing enough of this beautiful energy into or upon the polluted conditioning in your subconscious mind, over time the pollution *will* be diluted. For some this may happen fast for others it may take longer but the old negative thinking *will* become weaker and weaker and eventually it will be gone replaced with powerful, happy, healthy, prosperous concepts. You will be a strong powerful magnet to money. Singing with Michele affects your whole brain and makes you a more powerful magnet. Do what Michele sings. Do it. Live the beautiful words this day, let our songs help you create wonderful todays for the rest of your beautiful life. Sing it. See it. Do it. Take action on your dreams and you too will Be a Magnet to Money…

YOUR FREE ENERGY SONG

This affirmation song repeated over and OVER AGAIN WILL HAVE YOU GLOWING WITH VITALITY AND ENERGY. REMEMBER IT IS ALL conditioning. Use these miraculous and simple MusiVation™ songs to have you absolutely focused and energized.

Simply type into your Internet Browser

www.MysticalSuccessClub.com/EnergySong

CONGRATULATIONS you have made it this far!

Before we continue to the next portion of this book we are going to reward you for your persistence. You have been brave and awake enough -or hungry enough-for these truths to work in your life to get this far... so keep reading. Even if this is new to you and seems silly or scares you a little, you are doing it scared so BRAVO!!! For your persistence we are gifting you with 2 more powerful MusiVation™ songs as MP3's and they are **Decision** and **Persistence.** These 2 Songs combined with the **Magnet to Money** and *I Am Energy* songs will renew your mind and also help you to keep going with Love, Enthusiasm, Clarity, Resilience and Energy! Simply type the link below into your Internet Browser to receive the songs. Or if this is an ebook version simply click on the link or copy and paste the link into your browser. You will receive these 2 powerful MusiVation™ songs by Bob Proctor and Michele as MP3's. So enjoy the Power these songs will give you...

YOUR FREE PERSISTENCE and DECISION SONGS

These affirmation songs repeated over and OVER AGAIN WILL HAVE YOU PERSISTING until you DO SUCCEED! REMEMBER IT IS ALL conditioning. Use these miraculous and simple MusiVation™ songs to change your mind conditioning.

Simply type into your Internet Browser
www.MysticalSuccessClub.com/PersistenceDecisionSong

The Power Of Decision

There's a single mental move that turns the Dark to Light!

These are true words and lyrics from the first song Michele and I wrote together called *Decision*. What is that single mental move that turns the dark to light? It is DECISION POWER!

**Fame and Fortune Stand there waiting.
They will never fade away. There both yours for the asking, but there's a price
you need to pay...**

Again lyrics from another MusiVation™ we wrote on Persistence. And what is the price you need to pay?

It's Persistence yes Persistence that shovels up the gold. Its Persistence yes Persistence that brings fame and fortune to hold...

True lyrics and powerful MusiVation™ songs to help you whenever you need to be clear when making a decision and to help you keep on keeping on. Persistence DOES build resilience. If you truly wish to Become A Magnet To Money you must be resilient.

Persistence combined with the power of Decision is like carbon is to steel. We have added an extra gift of both these songs as MP3 downloads so that you can listen to these 2 songs every day along with the Magnet To Money and I Am Energy songs.

Some of these new lessons on Persistence and Decision are from our 7 CD MusiVation™ program titled **"New Paradigms"**. Once these two subjects are truly understood your life will change so rapidly and with such passion that all your actions will seem as if Grace was involved every step of the way. Grace will be your experience, for when we are focused and go for it in life no matter what the present circumstances, things will shift and everything we require in life to have our goals and life long wishes show up!

So let's start with DECISION because none of the success and money we desire is magnetized to us until we know what we want and we have made a Committed DECISION to have what we want!!

Once a decision has been made all will come to our aid to fulfill our goals and worthy ideals. Making a decision is a real commitment and Spirit that is us, as us, KNOWS when we have made a real committed **YES** to what we want.

Making a decision must never be based I will TRY that, but only if this happens first etc. There are no tries, ifs or buts on the road to success and certainly not in real decision making. If it scares us, well then we do it scared and if something does not scare and excite us at the same time then it's not really Big enough a dream. The things that shift our consciousness are always a little scary. This is a GOOD thing for we are growing and working outside of our old paradigm. We are building a new paradigm. Our old paradigms hate for us to change!

A young couple came to one of our live events in Singapore. This lovely young couple were newly weds and wanted to own their own home. They have every right to want to start their new lives together in the comfort of their own home. Especially because they both worked from home and environment is vitally important for consciousness. They were the same way as most of us are when we look only at the present appearances and make a decision based on appearances only.

They said, *"We do not have the money and we are pretty sure we will not be able to get a loan from a bank."*

Bob said, *"Make a decision that you WILL own your own home and the way clear will be made to you. Go and look at homes now and get clear on what you actually want."* Within three weeks this beautiful young couple called our office in Kuala Lumpur and said they were sending us a photograph of their new home they now owned.

You see once they had truly made a decision that they WOULD own their own home they met with a real estate agent *(they had actually met at the event)* who not only helped them find their perfect home but also a bank to loan them the money.

So you see the way *how* is never our worry the way how will appear once we have made a REAL DECISION to go for it. Things that before looked impossible now become possible. Do not ask God how this works take action and make a decision. This young couple took action by attending the event and the rest happened by law as it always does when we make a decision and take positive action.

Yes there is a single mental move you can make which in a millisecond will solve enormous challenges for you. It has the potential to improve almost any personal or business situation you will ever encounter and it can literally propel you down the path to incredible success. We have a name for this magic mental activity. What is it? You got it now, DECISION...Listen to this song and really get emotionally involved with the lyrics that were written just for *you.*

The world's most successful people share a common quality. They make decisions and rarely if ever change their minds. Yes decision makers go to the top and those who do not make decisions seem to go nowhere. Think about it...

Decisions or lack of them are responsible for the breaking or making of careers.

Individuals who have become very proficient in making decisions without being influenced by the opinions of others are the same people whose annual incomes fall into the six, seven and eight figure category. The person who has never developed the mental strength to make these vital moves is relegated to the lower income ranks their entire commercial career. And more often than not their life becomes little more than a dull boring existence.

It's not just your income that is affected by decisions. Your whole life is dominated by this power. The health of your mind and body, the well being of your family, your social life, the type of relationships you develop, are all dependent upon your ability to make sound decisions. Most of us will not often make decisions on our own, many individuals look first to what others will think of their choices. This is not freedom. ONLY YOU know what you want so only YOU should be the one making decisions about your own life. As long as what you decide is not hurting yourself or others GO FOR IT. Especially if what you want is helping educate your mind and spirit then say YES to these things. Let's repeat this ...

No one but YOU knows what is best for you.

You would think anything as important as decision making, when it has such far reaching power, would be taught in every school, but it's not. And to compound the problem, decision making is not only missing from the curriculum from almost all of our formal educational institutions, it has been left out of virtually all training and human resource development programs in our corporate world. At this point you could be asking yourself, "*How is a person expected to develop this mental ability?*" Well, there is an answer for you. You must do it on your own. And you've already begun by thinking about and digesting this information. This message is causing you to become more aware of the importance of decisions.

There's an excellent book that you might want to add to your library. It has some very powerful information between the covers. It's called "*Decision Power"* by Harvey Kaye. It's published by Prentice Hall. Kaye's book has a subtitle, '*How to Make Decisions with Confidence.*' That's the only way to make decisions. Don't make your decisions and then worry about whether you're doing the right thing. It is important to understand that it's not difficult to learn how to make wise decisions. With the proper information and by subjecting yourself to certain disciplines you can become a very proficient and effective decision maker.

And remember, it is the people who do become effective at decision making who receive a big share of the world's rewards.

Decision making is definitely a worthwhile subject to study and a mental discipline *you can* master.

Decision making could be compared to a number of mental disciplines like thinking, Imagineering, meditating or concentrating. Each one, when developed, brings with it tremendous rewards. The person who makes the decision to strengthen these mental muscles receives as their reward what is often considered a charmed life. You can virtually eliminate conflict and confusion in your life by becoming proficient in making decisions. Decision making brings order to your mind. And of course this order is reflected in your objective world, your results. James Allen, the great Victorian author, might have been thinking of decisions when he wrote, "*We think in secret and it comes to pass. Environment is but our looking glass."*

No one can see you making decisions, but they can always see the *results* of your decisions. The person who fails to develop this ability, to make decisions, is doomed because indecision sets up internal conflicts which can, without warning, escalate to all out mental and emotional wars. Psychiatrists have a name to describe these internal wars, it is *ambivalence.* The oxford dictionary tells us that ambivalence is *"The coexistence in one person of opposite feelings toward the same objective".* You do not have to be the brightest person in town and you certainly do not require a doctors degree in psychiatry to understand you are going to have a bit of difficulty in your life by permitting your mind to remain in an ambivalent state for any period of time.

The person who does permit it to exist will become very despondent and virtually incapable of any type of productive activity. It is obvious that anyone who finds themselves in such a mental state is not living; at best they are merely existing. A decision or a series of decisions would change everything. A very basic law of the universe is; create or disintegrate. Indecision causes disintegration. How often have you heard a person say, "*I don't know what to do*?" How often have you heard your self say, "*What should I do?*"

Think about some of the indecisive feelings you and virtually everyone else on this planet experience from time to time. Love them/leave them. Leave/Stay. Do it/don't do it. Go to work/Watch TV. Buy it/don't buy it. Say it/don't say it. Tell them/don't tell them. Everyone, on occasion, has experienced these feelings of ambivalence.

So make decisions based on what YOU WANT and then do not change your mind and do not let the appearances or other people influence you.

**If you want it and it is good for you
Make a Decision and go for it...**

Persistence

Now to share with you another powerful lesson, this time on **Persistence...**

Another person who has aptly demonstrated how far persistence can take you is Charlie Boswell. Boswell is a Birmingham, Alabama business man, sales man, author, and golfer. He holds numerous national and international golf championships. But what really distinguishes him is that he is blind. That's right. Charlie Boswell lost his sight after being blown off a tank in the Second World War. Selling, golfing, and writing are all the pursuits Boswell has engaged in since his tragic mishap.

Do you think Charlie Boswell is persistent?

Well do you?

If you were to compare an entrepreneurial or sales career to any in the entertainment industry, you would find that every actor or actress holds a dream of becoming a star. Every entrepreneur or sales person holds a dream. However as an entrepreneur or sales person you have a much greater control over your destiny. There's no capricious director or casting agent who can put their foot on the brake of your progress. You alone decide to quit or to continue when those inevitable mountains loom up on the road to your success.

Every industry has entrepreneurs and sales people and speakers and trainers. After every star there are at least twenty amateurs. 20% of the sales people take home 80% of the commissions. The beautiful aspect of sales is that you decide to which percent you will belong. And in the final analysis as an entertainer you must keep this beautiful truth firmly planted in your mind, that even the capricious directors and casting agents of our world are **always** overruled by the laws of our universe.

Whatever you can conceive and believe, through persistence, you must achieve.

Entrepreneurial situation or no, decide right now to be one of those people who make it happen. To be one of the group who receives the lion share of the profits and career success. Understand that to join this select group of big producers you must begin your persistence exercises *now.*

Make persistence your most well developed mental muscle. Persistence cannot be replaced by any other quality. Superior skills will not make up for it. A well rounded, formal education cannot make up to replace it. Nor will calculated plans nor a magnetic personality. When you are persistent you will become a leader in your career and industry.

There is a piece of literature written many years ago which illustrates that point perfectly. It was written by Calvin Coolidge. It's called "Persistence".

"Nothing in the world can take the place of persistence. Talent will not. Nothing is more common than unsuccessful people with talent. Genius will not. Unrewarded genius is almost a proverb. Education will not. The world is full of educated derelicts. Persistence and determination alone are omnipotent"

The slogan 'Press on' has solved and will solve the problems of the human race. The people who never tackled a mountain who perpetually wander in the foothills most of their lives have without even realizing it lied to themselves and everyone else who would listen so often and for so long that they are no longer even aware of what they are doing. They say they are content with their results. They will say that climbing a mountain is not important to them and that they are getting by just fine the way they are. Odds are they secretly started to climb the mountain years ago and got scared. They hit the terror barrier, quickly retreated to the comfort zone, and have been hiding behind their own false rational ever since. They frequently justify their mediocre performance with statements like, *"Why should I go all out? When I get there the boss will just want more."* These poor, non-productive individuals are lost, or at best misguided.

IF you are not able to wake these people up then PLEASE, make certain that you do not permit them to pull you into their trap. You do not want to catch what they have. In fact, when you come in contact with these poor souls let them serve as a triggering mechanism to mentally double your commitment to yourself to become more persistent. The Webster dictionary has this to say about persistence, *"To continue especially in spite of opposition or difficulty.'* Simple and true!

One of the most powerful speeches ever given was by the world renowned orator Sir Winston Churchill and the whole speech consisted of only three words.

Never Give up! Never Give up! Never Give up!

And Churchill knew what that really meant. He had a whole nation relying on him during the Second World War. To this point we have had something to say about persistence and about those who have developed it and the necessity for persistence. But there's something missing in this message.

How to? How do you become persistent?

That's a good question! Persistence is never developed by accident. You are not born with it and you cannot inherit it. And there is no one in the entire world that can develop persistence for you. Persistence is as interwoven with success as the chicken is with the egg.

And I'm talking about real success, as it's covered on one of the CD's on our MusiVation™ "New Paradigms" CD program we made on Success.

Ultimately persistence becomes a way of life, but that's not where it begins. To develop the mental strength, *persistence*, you must first really want something. You have to want something so much that it becomes a heated desire, a passion in your belly. You must fall in love with the idea, yes literally fall in love with the idea. (Or as we like to say rise in love) You have to magnetize yourself to every part of the idea. Then persistence will be automatic. The very idea of not persisting will become hateful and anyone who even attempted to take your dream away from you or stop you or slow you down would be in serious trouble. Difficulties, obstacles, and mountains will appear in one form or another and sometimes our own minds will make molehills into mountains but because of persistence they will be defeated every time.

Alright. Where does this leave you? It leaves you at the crossroads that every self-help book, every motivational program, and every seminar leads to.

Now we are getting back to how important Decision making is so that you can Be A Magnet To Money.

You must decide what you want!

WHAT DO YOU WANT?

Find out what you really, *really* want, way down deep inside and go for it...or you'll remain in the foothills forever with all the *what if* folks.

Very few people have admitted to themselves that THIS is what I want. This is what I really want and **I'm prepared to give my life for it.** That last statement may cause you to sit up and say, "*Wait a minute, this*

Proctor fellow must be mad, give my life for it?" And that's fine, but you must seriously think about it.

Why?

Because you are already giving your life for what you are doing.

What are you doing?

What are you trading your life for?

Are you making a fair trade?

Remember, whatever you are doing was your decision. Or was it? Or *was* it?

You could possibly be one of those poor people who have been wandering in the foothills leaving the decisions of where you are going and what you are doing with your life to other people. Just following, always following. That is where most people live. If that is the case, that's OK. Don't let it bother you for one more valuable second of your marvelous life. Forgive yourself and that way of life. Just let it go forever.

Treat this lesson on persistence as your wake up call. This red hot message on persistence will help you get out of the foothills and lead you to the very top of the mountain, all the way to the summit. It's not a chair lift, it will not make the climb any easier. You'll still attract the necessary challenges and they'll come to strengthen you, but this lesson will definitely make the climb to the top of the mountain a lot more fun. It will also help you develop a granite, strong attitude and certainty; the inner knowing **that you will get to the top.** The summit will be yours and the view from the top is going to be *awesome.* It will be reward enough for all the challenges you overcame.

Creative Visualization

The following information about visualization is powerful!

Why?

Because it works!

This is one of the most powerful ways to use the Law of Attraction for creating what you want to experince into your beautiful life. Let's share with you a real example from Bob's and my own experience about the power of visualization, and then share with you some techniques to do this for yourself. We've had many extraordinary things happen when we've used visualization. It's absolutely magical and fascinating... Our sub-conscious mind thinks in pictures and patterns. When we visualize, our sub-conscious mind doesn't know if it's real or if it's not. Neuroscientists have proven this in recent years. If we see a photograph of a car our mind thinks IT is an actual *real* three dimensional object. The sub-conscious mind cannot differentiate between a real car and a picture of a car.

The following story is a great example of how visualization worked for us. We were in Malaysia working together in Kuala Lumpur doing seminars and writing songs. We went to the middle of the city where they have a huge out door stage and we were writing a song together called *"Motivation for the Nation"* which in Bahasa Malaysia is *"Motivasi Untuk Bangsa."* We visualized we would have our song performed to an audience of *over* fifteen thousand and that this audience would also be singing along. We knew to add *over* because then we were not limiting the Unlimited Power. The thought of the Light and Power behind that many people singing together was *awesome.* It would be such a positive experience for all who were there. Now remember, we hadn't even finished writing the song, let alone recording it. We were on the stage visualizing fifteen thousand people and Bob always says that whatever you originally come up with, whether it's money or whatever, double it. So we doubled it and said it was to an audience of *over thirty thousand*.

Move forward in time to New Year's Eve ten months later. In 1996, there were three hundred musicians and dancers performing our song on that same stage to an audience of over fifty thousand people who were all singing along. Our song was played on national radio and the music video we created was on TV every day. The Prime Minister of Malaysia had chosen our song, by an Aussie and a Canadian, to help bring in the New Year for his country and yes, we will repeat, there were over fifty thousand people bringing in the New Year singing our positive Light filled song.

What we had done was record the song with Michele and many of the country's biggest singing pop stars and it ended up being a very popular song. In fact, it is still being played. It was sort of an anthem for the country. That came about because of creative visualization. So when you visualize, always see it happening NOW and do not ask *how* it will happen. Once you have made a decision on what you want and have visualized it, ideas and opportunities will arise. THEN, you are to immediately begin taking *action* on these ideas and opportunities.

Always ask for what you want or something even better, and always add, "*I give thanks that this happened in ways which were for my highest good and for the highest good of everyone involved,*" because the Infinite Intelligence knows what we want, better than we know what we want and always knows the how to. That's just the way it is.

So how to do this?

To start we have to *feel*. Really get into the emotions of *how you would feel* having the success you desire. Whatever your "it" is, ask yourself first, *"How would I really FEEL if this were to happen in my life?"*

You may be surprised as it may be a feeling of peace relief, or simply unbridled passion and of course gratitude. If you cannot imagine how you would feel go back into your memory and think of a time when you had achieved something that was really wonderful. Get yourself into that love vibration where you feel very happy and then visualize what it is you want as if it had already been experienced. When we focus and visualize our BIG PICTURE, we can then take the necessary action as we are guided to have this beautiful picture be our experience. If we were given a jigsaw puzzle and were not first shown the actual finished picture, it would be very challenging to find which piece went where. We may still be able to achieve this, however, it could take much longer and we may give up before the puzzle was completed.

When we can actually see and rehearse it in our mind and know what it is we want to create *first*, it is then much easier and more fun to put the pieces together. What a feeling of accomplishment and fulfillment we get when we have finished and are putting that very last puzzle piece into place.

Ask yourself...

- What is my big picture?

- How does it look?

- How does it feel?

- How do I feel?

- What do I look like?

- Who am I with?

Write down now, on the lines below; and in as much detail as possible, your dream of succeeding in your career or any area of your life and see it as if you had already experienced it happening.

See it, feel it, touch it, breathe it in. Write it down NOW as if IT HAS already been achieved.

I am so joyously happy and deeply grateful now that...

_____
_____
_____
_____
_____
_____
_____
_____
_____
_____
_____
_____
_____
_____
_____
_____
_____
_____
_____
_____

Excellent! Now that you have written your vision down, put all of your attention on your dream, on this beautiful picture. Attention simply means – to stretch toward. This is your intention, *to stretch toward your vision.* Visualizing will not only stretch you toward what it is you desire to experience, this tool of the mind will also have it come to you. You WILL meet together in this third dimension at the right place and the right time. It is very important to visualize what you want.

What is really happening is the veil of illusion will dissolve and what you wanted will appear, as it was always there, you just could not see it. Wondrous and powerful images will begin to appear in your physical world when you do this. Ideas will come to you, the right influential people, great opportunities, and so much good.

Do this repeatedly and then it will become your actual experience.

As was mentioned earlier when Bob spoke of an MSI board, do another board with your goals laid out in pictures. We call this your Magnetic Creative Visualization Board.

Get a large piece of poster cardboard from your local office supply house and after completion paste this up on a wall in your office or living area. Paste onto it pictures of all the things you want to have and wish to achieve. For example, go to a car dealer and have someone take a photo of you sitting in the car of your dreams. Then have this blown-up and add an affirmation to it. *"I give thanks for my beautiful new car. I love driving safely in this luxurious machine."*

You can do this with anything; travel, new office computers, homes, companionship, money, employment, vacation destinations, etc.,

Write this affirmation on your board. *"I am so grateful that all of my dreams have come true and I am now doing what I love to do and I am highly paid doing what I love. I am now easily able to experience the things in life that make me more comfortable"* Then add what it is you do, as if you are <u>now</u> doing it. Some of our readers may be authors, trainers, MLM folk, actors, writers, others musicians who see themselves winning awards, etc. I am pretty sure now that you get the *picture*... excuse the pun.

YOUR FREE AUDIO PROGRAM MAGNETIC CREATIVE VISUALIZATION

Here is a truly powerful program that is another FREE GIFT. This program will allow you to understand in more detail the power of visualization and has an actual visualization so you can rehearse in your mind what you want to create.

Simply type into your Internet Browser
www.MysticalSuccessClub.com/MagneticCreative

The Power Of Meditation

Practicing Meditation forms a most important part of our work in becoming a Magnet To Money, Success, Joy and Peace of Mind. The reason we say practicing is because Eternity meditates us... we call it practicing meditation until we have the real experience of total oneness.

Now because the purpose of this book is to give you tools to assist you in attracting wealth, we are not going to now delve into the Power of Meditation. Why? Because if we desire to truly move ahead and have wealth flowing and become part of our experience always we must tap into that which sustains all. (This will be discussed in more depth in Part Two, *The Sea Of Unlimited Consciousness.*) However, this important topic must be added to some degree in Part One as the power of meditation is often overlooked. If we wish to truly connect with our higher self and not get into thinking it is our own mind that is creating or attracting what we want then this chapter on meditation will assist you to look more deeply. This chapter will teach those who have never meditated before and will remind those who do practice meditate – its' awesome power. When we practice meditation we are consciously connecting, in the silence to our Higher Power.

Although there are many ways taught to achieve silence through meditation practice we will share with you some ideas that will meet your needs very nicely indeed.

Create your own space where you will meditate. Clean this area really well as this will release old energies because when we meditate it is best to have clean energy. Buy a brand new mat on which to sit. Light a beautiful candle as you can use the candle flame to focus your attention. A candle *does* bring in good energy into your space as does traditional incense. A flower or some kind of lush green plant is also good. If you do not live alone ask your room mate or partner to please respect that this is your special place. Of course to actually sit outdoors on the earth is always clean and wonderful but always designate a special place where you live to meditate in your home and meditate alone.

Do not meditate in bed as you will add too much energy to your bed and may find it difficult to sleep as meditation gives us more energy. Meditation is not meant to make you sleepy; it is a much focused practice. Visualization exercises, as mentioned earlier, are OK to do in bed as you can then flow into a positive sleep, filled with pictures that you can take into your dream time.

Once you have your meditation space prepared and cleaned sit down on your mat (lotus style if you can) sit up straight, arms out to your sides and breathe in through your nose deeply, hold it and then exhale slowly through your mouth. Keep doing this until you feel peaceful. As you are now sitting quietly place your attention centered somewhere between the eyes and a little above, and take some word that is powerful to you, you will know it when you try some words out. LOVE, BLISS, GOD, SPIRIT, BEAUTY and ponder the word you choose. Some of my mantra's are, *As a wave is one with the ocean I am One with God, As a ray of sun is one with the sun I am one with God, I Love God, or God's Grace is flowing through me, I am now a clear instrument for God's Grace,* or AUM or OM, use only one power word if that suits you better. You do not have to be religious to do this. This is about focus and connection and meditation practices will strengthen your mind. Replace the word God with Love if this feels more comfortable to you.

As you are sitting and focused on your power word, Love, Heart etc, your thoughts *will* wander off, when this happens gently refocus your mind back to the same mantra or word. Feel no impatience with yourself or frustration. No matter how many times your mind wanders, bring it back to that one word.

If you do this simple method, eventually, you will find that outside, intruding thoughts will cease, and you will be able to sit quietly in a peaceful state. It may take days or it may take months to acquire this steadiness of mind, but it will come if you have patience and are consistent.

At first do not attempt to remain quiet for more than five minutes or so unless we feel like it. After a couple of weeks meditate for ten minutes and so on until we can sit comfortably for much longer periods. We are doing this to have a conscious realization of our unity with Spirit or to make contact with God. We are not attempting to see "light" or to have "experiences". If they do come just refocus the mind, as if we become too fascinated with these "experiences" we could lose sight of the original intention and make way too much of them. Keep it simply. KISS – "Keep It Simple and Spiritual", and remember to smile as we wish to bring a happy vibration to our meditation time. I call smiling my *Happy Meditation*.

After we have had a few minutes of meditation and have achieved that feeling of peace, joy and unity with the Universe give thanks get up and go about our day. It is recommended that we do this three or four times a day. First thing in the morning, at lunchtime (noon is best) and then at night (best when sun is setting a powerful time to connect with God's presence) and then at midnight or just before we are to go to bed.

When we first begin this practice, perhaps just meditate for five minutes three times a day or for some perhaps just having the intention to connect with your soul for two – three minutes say four or five times a day will help. This will be a great start.

Why?

Ultimately, meditating three or four times a day even if for just a few minutes each time will bring us to a place where we will be focused and unified with the Divine Presence all day, whether asleep or awake.

Even if you are agnostic, look at meditation as physicians do. It has been documented that people who meditate regularly have low blood pressure and generally are healthier, happier human beings. So do it even if the word God is not your thing. Put a smile on your face as you sit down to meditate as this DOES help your mind find peace. Do whatever you can to put yourself into a happy mindset before you sit down.

As mentioned, this chapter is a simple way of learning to practice meditation. Before we truly experience real silence we are all only practicing meditation. But every time we do this we DO raise our consciousness, even if we do not realize it. In time we will feel better and clearer and definitely less clogged or stressed. It is NOT to be taken in an overly serious tone, focused yes, but not so serious. Oscar Wilde said *"Life is too serious to be taken seriously,"* so LIGHTEN UP! Focus your attention and feel happiness and gratitude. This way it is a simple and easy way to begin to practice, but do not underestimate its power. And if you do not at first FEEL any connection or peace of mind that is OK. Just having the intention to consciously connect and feel the presence of God will eventually create in you peace, joy and everything good will begin flowing your way.

WHY?

Because at least for a few minutes a day you have chosen to get out of the way and let God in. As you delve into longer meditations and find a way that suits you best -and there are many different ways to learn meditation- your life and physical well being WILL radically change for the better. Oh yes it will.

If you are interested in delving more into consciousness and meditation please DO read Part Two.
If you are having a challenge with your meditation practice, do not give up, allow these loving and all wise words by the great soul Paramahansa Yogananda to assist you, *"Your trouble with meditation is that you don't persevere long enough to get results. That is why you never know the power of a focused mind. If you let muddy water stand still for a long time, the mud will settle at the bottom and the water will become clear. In meditation, when the mud of your restless thoughts begins to settle, the power of God begins to reflect in the clear waters of your consciousness. You will become a smile millionaire."*

I LOVE that. Yes let us become Smile Millionaires! Always remember to smile sincerely and breathe… Life is magical, oh yes it is!

YOUR FREE PRACTICE OF MEDITATION VIDEO

Here is a truly powerful program that is another FREE GIFT. This program will allow you to learn how to become one with the Inner Beauty and Power that is within each and everyone of us and awaken your Oneness with the Divine Presence.
Simply type into your Internet Browser

www.MysticalSuccessClub.com/PracticeOfMeditationVideo

Diagram Of OUR AMAZING MIND

By Dr. Thurman Fleet 1934

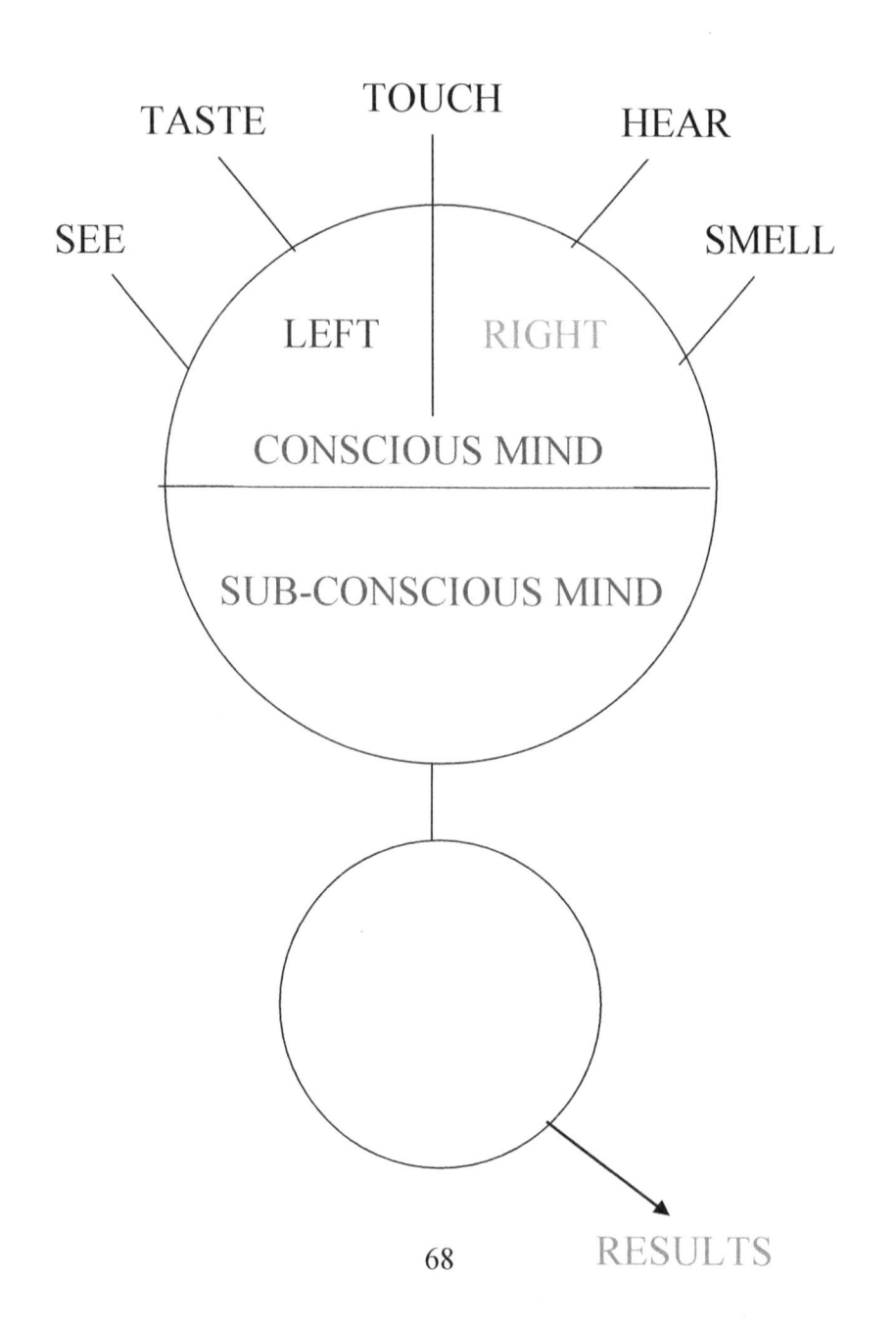

TASTE — TOUCH — HEAR

SEE — SMELL

LEFT | RIGHT

CONSCIOUS MIND

SUB-CONSCIOUS MIND

RESULTS

THE MIND

Having an understanding of the mind is a vitally important aspect in your education of becoming a Magnet To Money. For those of our readers *who do* know this information let this be a reminder of how your mind does indeed work. We can NEVER ever get enough respect for the mind especially in a world filled with other minds that are still asleep to the Universal Laws.

So now let us cover the mind.

The Conscious Mind

Now, imagine if you will that the diagram on the page above is your mind cut into halves. The first half is your *Conscious Mind* - where only one-sixth of your thinking is actually done; here we experience our physical senses of *sight, taste, touch, hearing* and *smell*. This is the part of you that thinks and reasons – your free will resides here. The conscious mind can accept or reject any idea. No person or circumstance can cause you to think about thoughts or ideas you do not choose. The *thoughts* you choose eventually determine the results in your life. All your experiences, including the negative and positive, originate in the conscious mind, or are taken in from an outside source such as another person or the media etc. As you accept a thought, it is impressed upon the second part of your personality. *"We DO become what we constantly think about."*

The Right & Left Side Of The Conscious Mind

Now let's cut the conscious mind in half. In one half we have the left side of the mind, which is our analytical or logical part of our conscious mind. This is where we think and form words and speech. The right side of our mind is our creative side. This is where we feel music, we don't just hear it. This is where inspiration for NEW ideas and the so - called magic happens. That Is why our *MusiVation*™ songs are so powerful as the lyrics (words) of the songs effects stimulation in the left side of our mind and the music and melody affects the right side of the mind, and then we have a whole brain experience. This enables the affirmations (Positive lyrics) to go directly into our sub-conscious mind. This is a fun and powerful way to get these positive thoughts to begin working for us right away. That is why without music, advertising agencies would *not* have the success they have, as the music jingles stay with us forever and therefore the advertisers' products also stay with us forever. So *now* we can advertise the things that we DO want into our mind...instead of what we don't want.

The Sub-Conscious Mind

Now to the next bottom-half of the mind, the *Sub-Conscious Mind*. This is where our sixth sense comes into play, plus this is where five-sixths of our thinking actually takes place. This part of you is certainly the most magnificent, for it is your power center. It functions in every cell of your body. Every thought your conscious mind chooses to accept, this part must accept. It has no ability to reject it. This part of you operates in an orderly manner. "By Law," it expresses itself through you, in feelings and action. Any thought you consciously choose to impress upon the sub-conscious over and over becomes fixed in this part of your personality. Fixed ideas will then continue to express themselves without any conscious assistance, until they are replaced. Fixed ideas are more commonly referred to as habits. The sub-conscious mind is the God-like part of you, referred to as Spirit. It knows NO LIMITS. Which means YOU have no limits. What a wonderful fact of life!! (*Remember that this, of course, is NOT how our mind or brain actually looks, you did not read this book to become a neurologist after all. We find it is simply an excellent and simple diagram for us to see the way the mind works.*)

The Body

Now let's talk about *how* we achieve results. The body is the physical representation of you, the material medium in the third dimension. It is merely the instrument of the mind, or the house we live in. The thoughts or images that are consciously chosen and impressed upon the sub-conscious - which is in every cell of our body - moves our body into action.

The actions we are involved in determine our results. We become almost self-propelled through the feelings our thoughts have stimulated and then we take action. So with positive thoughts going in, positive actions will always follow.

1 – Thoughts come first
2 – Feelings come next
3 – Actions come next because of what we have thought and felt
4 – The action we take leads us to results.

It is truly amazing. It NEVER ceases to fascinate when we see how it works in people's lives.

It is VITAL for us to understand that even if our mind has been conditioned with feelings of negativity, *we can* change our thoughts to change the conditions in our lives. We cannot blame anyone else for the conditions in our life, as everything we have been taught is just a condition, and the people that taught us were also taught that same condition. Our past is not a precedent for our future.

This is why if your Mother was a school teacher or your Father say a policeman you may also become a teacher or a police officer. This is fine if you *want* to be with all of your heart in one of these fine professions, but not if you want to be an entrepreneur running your own show or an actor or musician. It is a waste of our life force and purpose to begin a career based solely because we think it will make our parents proud or because we think it is expected of us. We have to live our own life, and WE CAN! So let's go onto our next topic, as it is our desire and intention, as previously stated, that by the time you have studied this book, you will be in such a high state-of-understanding these great truths, you will become **unstoppable!**

Now let's find out *how* to STOP the thoughts we do not want...

Think Good Positive Thoughts

You cannot think of two things at the same time so whenever a negative thought comes in, remember you have control of your thoughts simply say STOP. Be quite for 60 seconds and then replace the other thought with a positive in the NOW thought!

Say out loud STOP whenever a negative thought crosses your mind. Once we know why we are thinking a negative thought we can say...

STOP...

The Terror Barrier Diagram
Bob Proctor designed this diagram via the original by Dr. Thurman Fleet 1934

Do not permit old conditioning to prevent you from performing new acts in an efficient and effective manner or from enjoying that which is your birthright.

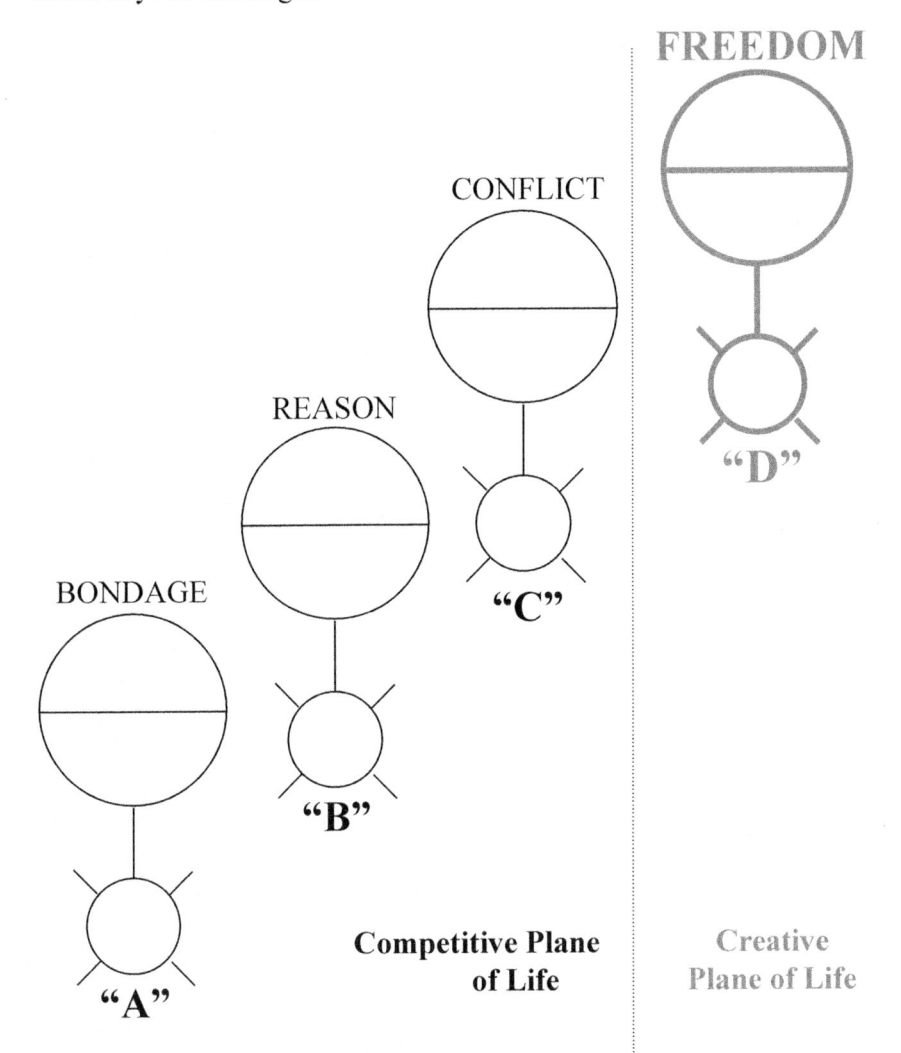

FREEDOM

CONFLICT

REASON

BONDAGE

"D"

"C"

"B"

"A"

Competitive Plane of Life

Creative Plane of Life

Go ahead and jump over that terror barrier, just do it. Even if you are scared, do it scared. JUMP!

The Terror Barrier

The previous diagram is again something Bob Proctor (www.BobProctor.com) put together based on Dr Fleet's original diagram. Now let us explain as clearly as possible *how* important it is to cross over this *illusion* Bob has named *The Terror Barrier*.

Have a look at the diagram above.

Now let's pretend your letter "A".

"A" is when we are in thought-bondage. Bondage can mean that <u>we don't know that we don't know</u>. We may not know what to do next with our life and feel a little confused and lost. Too many fears seem to have us feeling stuck. We don't feel excited when we get up in the morning, we may even be doing things to self-sabotage our success without realizing it, like turning up late for appointments, being too tired to finish that last chapter of a book we are writing etc; we always seem to have a legitimate excuse all ready to go as to why we were late or did not finish a project or make that important call. Perhaps you are a writer, and you don't bother sending your scripts out anymore, and if you do send them, you may never follow-up. If this sounds like you, there is nothing to fear because YOU CAN get over this.

You then move up to the "B" level/Reason.

At the "B" level we start to have reason. We wake up. The catalyst for this wake up could be any number of things. This book may be your wake up call. Maybe someone begins to believe in you. Something happens. Your mind begins to shift to the *I CAN* attitude and at last you begin to experience clarity and reason. You start feeling happy again and positive, and you say, *"That's it! I'm going to do it. Nothing can stop me."* You're so excited and then...

You move in to "C" Level/Conflict

"C" level is where our mind begins to revert back to its old way of thinking and causes conflict with our new positive plans for Success. Look at the diagram again. Conflict comes up. How does that conflict come up? OK, the number one conflict can be our old paradigm. And this simply means our old conditioning, our old belief system from our sub-conscious mind, begins speaking to us and says *"You can't do this, what were you thinking, your not good enough, you don't have enough talent. Who are you kidding? It's too much to handle."* **Do not listen** to this voice; it is just old stinking-thinking patterns. It is not the truth. So what do you do with it? Say STOP and shift your focus back to what you want.

They may not even be your own thoughts! The conflict may come and disturb your newfound reason from another source. It could be a parent, our mate, or even our best friend or the person you are sitting next to on a plane or subway. We are psychic beings and we do pick up others thoughts and vibrations.

So you have this new idea and new found passion about your life and career. You are all excited and share your new found wisdom and ideas with your spouse or friends. As was stressed in the chapter on Decision... no one but YOU can decide what you want. Our loved ones think they are helping by discouraging our dreams because they want us to not be disappointed or feel dejected. They simply do not understand the Universal Laws of Creativity and are living in fear. One of these well meaning loved ones may say, *"But honey you have a good job now and responsibilities";* or *"Why are you spending all your time and money on this pipe dream better off quit now so you don't get hurt."* You see this is simply *their* old paradigm and their fears, it is not their fault. They love you but they just don't know the truth. When we have an inspiration to change our lives and live our dreams into realty it is literally our higher-self directing us and we *must* follow our creative dreams or we will shrivel up and either die or at least feel dead.

Since that is no way to live, STOP those negative ideas that are causing conflict. In fact, do not share your newfound reason and excitement with anyone unless they are people who will encourage and support you.

Move to Level "D" The Creative Plane of Life

This is the time when we have to be the bravest, my friend. It's when we have to shoot over the Terror Barrier. There is no competition in life. It's you out there doing it and no one can stop you. <u>You can't take away from any body else if you want to be successful and make great money doing what you love to do.</u> There is plenty for everyone! All you can do is add to the magic that we're all part of.

Have a look at the diagram again. There isn't really a barrier. It's only an imaginary line; it's all just an "imaginary" boundary in our minds. Go to the creative plane of life. Jump over into the land of creative freedom. It is so vital for us to not ask for the opinions of others, unless they truly know what we feel and are there to help and support our vision. Don't ask for advice from someone about your career and goals unless that person has done it successfully themselves. We get out of conflict by jumping *over* the (imaginary, self-imposed) Terror Barrier. Do not be afraid as it is only an illusion, and even if we are scared, then let us DO IT SCARED...but please just DO IT.

Another great idea is to say. *"It is not fear I am feeling, it is actually excitement and I simply did not recognize the feeling. Yes I am excited."* If you still feel some conflict come up, simply say, *"OK, this has been explained to me. The anxiety I am feeling is only in my mind it is the imaginary Terror Barrier. I know it is only my old ideas that are making me feel this fear because I am going for something big and it feels different to go for something so BIG. My dream is beautiful. I deserve to be successful and live my own life. I'm going to jump through the fear and go for it."*

Be persistent for a little bit longer. You may only be five minutes away from having your dream come true. Smile and say *"You can't trick me again you are not real.* ***STOP!*** Study this chapter over again and again until the fear is gone. Read this book at least four times and then reread it every month.

Another extremely powerful way to release fear is to get organized and learn about the power of a daily action list! When we are taking action with focus we don't have time to ponder the *ifs* that lead to fear.

YOUR FREE BOOK WRITING COURSE

We have included Michele's full video and audio Book Writing Course. This is an amazing system to assist those who feel they wish to produce a product, audio, video or book. Even if you do not feel you wish to write a book or create products at this time, please be open minded and watch the videos.

You may be very surprised at what you will learn about yourself and what you TRULY wish to create in your life, anything is possible...

www.MysticalSuccessClub.com/BookWritingSystem

The Power of a
DAILY ACTION LIST!

It has been proven in many research studies that people who write down their goals DO achieve them and when we also add the power of the mind, decision and persistence with a planned daily action list, well then my friend you will be a legend in your career. It seems so simple, however not many people will stick to a plan or even write down any goals. Create a BIG GOAL and every day you work, follow a positive action list. If you took action on even just one idea that you have received in this book your income will increase and your life will improve. So just imagine how much you can attract and create if you followed all of these ideas? WOW!

You will become irresistible to Money and Success.

If you were told if you did this daily action list every single day for the next 30 days that there would be a pot of gold waiting for you, your dream coming to life, would you do it?

YES, I am sure that you would. But many people say they will and then after a few days give up. Be one of the 3% group who NEVER GIVES UP.

When you first begin doing a daily action list you will find that projects in the past that seemed impossible to complete will now be completed and *ahead of time.* Your life will begin to have clarity and order and your success will begin flowing. You will be able to accomplish more with less time. No more doing things just to be busy. Doing this list WILL help you in ways that will seem miraculous.

Instructions

Write down your daily action list at night. You will do your daily list every evening for thirty days. Why write your list in the evening? Because as you are sleeping your sub-conscious mind will help you attract opportunities and creative ideas for those actions to come to fruition. It will help you be self propelled to take positive enthusiastic action the next day.

Tape your action list up on a wall where you work each day and highlight each action that is completed with a bright yellow highlighter after each is completed. We recommend you write down the hardest action first. You will find that making that call you have been putting off early in the morning after you have meditated and completed your spiritual practices will no longer scare you. Calling anybody for any reason will now seem like fun. Doing the actions that you don't like or that intimidate you *first* will help you gain light and power. *You know* those things that you keep putting off.

Research has proven that doing this will accelerate your dreams into action faster than you could ever realize. You will no longer be a procrastinator; you will be a doer not a wishful thinker. A quickening of good will begin to appear in your life. If you have not completed the six items on your list by the end of the evening add what was not completed to the next day's list. Do not beat yourself up too much (maybe a little bit ☺) if you haven't done them all. Say to yourself, *"This is so simple. It is worth it to me. I will have clarity. I will know what I've done. I will stay clear. I will be getting things done that are helping me achieve my dreams towards success. I am committed to taking these positive actions on my daily action list. I know that each detail is just as important as any other."*

You know the saying, *"God is in the details"*! Do each action with total focus and impeccability. Doing each

80

action with love, focus and impeccability will also keep you mindful. If you find you are not doing all of the things on your DAILY LIST, perhaps you've put up one action step that is too big to be one action. **This is not goal setting; these are actions to help you complete your goals.**

Here is an example of a goal as apposed to an action: *"Today I will create a website and put a streamed video of me on my website for customers to get to know me and our services."* This is a goal, NOT an individual action. Instead we recommend one action towards this website goal could be, *"Buy domain name today"* for the next day, *"Find web designer"*, for the following day, *"Get a photograph of myself looking amazing for the homepage of my website"*, for the fourth day, *"Hire a camera and video myself sharing who I am and how my service has so many benefits"*, for the fifth day *"Have video compressed at local video editors to stream onto my website"*, and sixth day *"Write copy for the home page,"* etc...

Beginning to get how this works?

Now with this example it could take a week to a month working on the preliminary action steps for completing your Website.

NOW can you see how working with a simple daily action list will have you in no time at all achieving the project you wish to start *and* complete. You don't list a project/goal as one item on your DAILY LIST. Instead, break it down into action steps.

By breaking down your goals into manageable pieces you will find that your six things will be very easy to do. DO NOT overwhelm yourself by putting more than six items on your DAILY LIST. Just do one thing at a time.

The reason we have indicated a numbered day (30 in total) for each DAILY LIST is because you will want to make sure that you do this list every single day for a full consecutive 30 days. That's right, seven days a week. This way it will become an easy thing to do and will no longer feel like a discipline. It will be just as easy as brushing your teeth and showering. It will become a new positive habit. After the initial 30 days, you can do four or five days a week if that is what you choose to do, however doing this list for the first time in a consecutive thirty days, will create an amazing NEW Habit, a new Positive Paradigm and increase your clarity and your results exponentially. You will FEEL SO GOOD about yourself *because* YOU DID IT!

If you do miss a day, you have to start over from day one. Even if it is at day twenty five, if you miss one day, you have to begin at Day One until a full thirty days is completed. You may be up to day twenty eight and miss it because of just feeling like you deserved a day off, however that is simply your old paradigm clicking back in again so forgive yourself and begin again at day one. Soon this will become a new habit that you will find gives you deep satisfaction and fulfillment. Yes, you WILL see definite positive results. You will know that this initial 30 days was well worth it as you will be so ahead in the game of life that it will literally feel miraculous. You can do this. Do it for you!!

Please do not cheat by making any justifications there is no point in cheating yourself that is just silly. This is YOUR LIFE and YOU are the one who is responsible for making YOUR LIFE WORK.

You deserve this for you!

So be excited and begin DAY ONE of your daily action list. I suggest you add one more thing to your list.

Today I serve another. This can be through a tithe, an act of kindness, a gift, a smile to a stranger etc.

The next page is a sample of a daily action list...

~ MY DAILY LIST ~

for:_____
(date)

I am so excited about becoming focused and doing my positive daily action list because I KNOW that taking these actions is definitely helping my dreams come true.

I LOVE doing these positive actions. It is easy for me to do my daily list one positive action at a time.

Positive Action #1

Positive Action #2

Positive Action #3

Positive Action #4

Positive Action #5

Positive Action #6

YOUR FREE DAILY ACTION AND TURBO CHARGED GOAL SETTING A PLANNER & AUDIO PROGRAM

Here is a truly powerful program that is another FREE GIFT. This program will allow you to go into more detail about how to take Action and set your Goals learn how to take positive focused Action in your life.

Simply type into your Internet Browser
http://www.MysticalSuccessClub.com/ActionPlanner

Responsibility

Take the following information on this page to heart because it can change your life for the better and help you become wealthier and more successful than you could ever dream presently. I thought of this back in January 2002 as I was researching why some people can work quite well in a particular job situation; however, when they took time to do their own thing, whether it was to write a book or get their websites together etc., they seemed to always fall short and never finish what they started. This was a puzzle to me, as I knew that these people had a deep desire to have their dreams come true and to wanted to be running their own business, doing their own thing.

Why then couldn't they ever finish or sometimes even start working on their dreams and projects? Why was this wonderful person wasting their precious time? WHY? Why were they not completing anything they started? Suddenly it dawned on me and it became crystal clear. People have been so ingrained to do work for *someone else* and the fear of being fired seems to be one of the reasons –and of course to pay the rent- that keeps them doing what they do each day from 9 to 5 or from 6 to 2 for those who work in restaurants or night shifts. I realized they were simply programmed to work only when they had been paid by someone else. What if they could change this pattern? Wouldn't that change their lives? Yes it would, so here is my advice! I KNOW it is simple and yet it works and will help you achieve success.

Are you ready?

TREAT *EVERY* ACTION YOU TAKE AS RESPONSIBLY AS IF YOU WERE BEING PAID $$$ Money $$$ TO DO IT!

Remember to be of service to others.

YOUR LIFE WILL CHANGE!

Remember your Daily Action List? Well, here is a reminder! Every single day make a list of a maximum of 6 things and DO THEM and pretend you are being paid $$ money $$ to do them and always remember you are in business to be of service to others.

Now onto a very important and vital topic to help with your success, Gratitude...

Gratitude & Appreciation

Gratitude is one of the most powerful forces in life because it is one of the many facets of love. When we understand this we find that gratitude will play a far greater part in our experience than could ever be totally realized in this physical consciousness.

The mistake most of us make is that we are only grateful for the good that *comes to us* instead of being grateful for the good *we now have* and be grateful for that which *we do want* before it appears. Let's find a deeper appreciation of all the so called little things in life. Take breathing for example. Breath is something we take for granted. Be grateful for the fact that we can breath without having to think about it. Some are not so fortunate. You can also write out on sticky notes thank you messages and put them all over your house. I discuss this more in part two.

Let's do a simple exercise right now to get into a place of gratitude and appreciation. Make a list of things and people right now that you are grateful for and appreciate. The power behind being grateful and being appreciative is beyond our human comprehension. It creates miracles and enormous success. Wonderful opportunities will seem to fall out of the sky into your lap.

Remember, success without fulfillment is empty and meaningless; *with* fulfillment it is pure bliss. So remember to always give thanks and appreciate all that you receive and experience!! EVERY night before going to sleep write in a special exercise book or note pad at least five things you were grateful for that day. Anything from having a hot shower, to arriving safely at a destination, a smile some stranger gave you or perhaps the name of a friend you appreciate who is in your life. Put a date on each page and at the end of the week read them all out loud. It is a very powerful exercise and will STOP you from indulging in the *poor me* game PLUS you will attract even more things into your life you can be grateful for.

I, _____, give thanks for all of this in my life and more.

- _____
- _____
- _____
- _____
- _____
- _____
- _____
- _____
- _____
- _____
- _____
- _____
- _____
- _____

What is Consciousness?

We have been talking a lot about prosperity consciousness but what *is* consciousness?

Soul, or Consciousness is our Higher Self! Joel S. Goldsmith the great mystic teacher said it perfectly," *The day will come when, if you know enough about Consciousness you can leave everything else alone, for in the word, 'Consciousness,' and the spiritual understanding of it, is contained all the knowledge that is to be known about God, man, and the universe."* Joel was Enlightened so he knew how to attempt to explain to the intellect what cannot be explained and so beautifully.

We who are on the spiritual path or seekers are always doing all we can to gain more *consciousness.* Again that word? Well before we go any further if any of what you have read so far on this topic sounds way too out there for you well no worries just skip it. Maybe you will come back to it at another time, BUT if you truly desire to have wealth AND fulfillment then please do your soul a favour and keep reading... And for those of you who deeply desire to learn more, you will devour Part Two in this volume about *The Sea of Unlimited Consciousness where you will learn how to melt down the ice and become aware of who you really are.*

When we speak of raising our awareness or gaining higher consciousness, what we are saying is we are doing our best to consciously connect with God so that we become one, there is no duality - we just don't know it. We may know it intellectually, but we don't know *it* unless we can *feel it* within. We are always striving to have more and more moments of pure bliss and knowingness. Only a few rare beings ever become completely Enlightened in this physical experience but luckily for us there are those rare beings who have attained and have done their best to teach us. Transmissions do go on and as we raise our awareness we slowly begin to melt away the ice and begin to feel our connection with Spirit. Oh our beautiful soul, what tales it can tell us when we are ready to listen...

That is when we truly begin to understand *that God is closer to me than breathing, closer than hands and feet. Eternity/God is inseparable and indivisible because we are one.*

Whether we believe this or not does not stop it from being true. Those who live in this realization *consciously* find that when any form of lack or so called opposition comes into their experience, it disappears. This is the REAL secret of life. The secret of the spiritual life. We are NOT speaking of religion, even though all religions do agree on this one point that *wherever we are God is.* When we meditate we are doing this to connect with our higher consciousness or soul. In the silence, this is where true consciousness is experienced. This is where we are alive in Spirit. Our inner vision begins to open and we hear, or feel, *the still small voice* of our soul. These are the true eyes that see. Some have been able to see with their eyes closed when in a meditative state.

This *still small voice* is our spiritual guide and it actually then goes beyond what we *think* intuition is. For true consciousness has no thought. It is pure knowingness. If we wish to begin to really get into more conscious awareness of our connection with Spirit we must meditate, which is why we added the chapter on basic meditation, because until we are in the silence we are only practicing meditation. In today's world where there are over six billion minds thinking and we are taking on *their* thoughts. Without going within to the silence we can find it very hard to focus our minds and this is one of the main reasons we get so stressed out and do our best to slip into something more comfortable like a collective coma by distracting our minds with hours upon hours of mesmerizing TV.

Most of the world is in a collective coma and they don't even know it. Fear and lack does not live in pure consciousness it only lives in duality.

One simple way to see whether we are rising in consciousness is to notice if we are becoming less reactionary. When we react our ego is still in power over our lives. When we notice that now we are an observer to what is going on rather than a reactor we are gaining awareness. Respond, be in the moment before we react and then our actions that follow will be right actions.

Another quote from the great mystic Joel S, Goldsmith," *If, on entering a new year, our consciousness is the same consciousness with which we came into the previous year, we can be sure of duplicating the previous year's experience. But if our consciousness has deepened and been enriched, the New Year will be enriched.*"

That says it all. Perhaps if Joel had been here at this time on the planet he would have also mentioned the film "Groundhog Day" for without more awareness or higher consciousness we DO live our life and each year the same way over and over again. Just the names change but the experiences remain the same. We however do not have to wait until a New Year to begin. We can begin right here and right now. Begin to meditate, stop watching so much TV and focus on Light, on conscious union with God. Indeed it is ALL about consciousness, and we will say it again... Remember to smile!

Intuition

To begin to explain in words the awesome power of our intuition is a true challenge. As discussed previously, intuition is part of *consciousness* but it is not pure consciousness. Developing our intuition is vitally important if we wish to be free and KNOW that we KNOW. Logic has nothing to do with intuition nor does so called *common sense.*

As we melt away the ice of duality we then tap deeply into the power of our intuition and we are clearly guided. Our life with this guidance, becomes a glorious, happy, and on purpose experience. Whenever we are doing mind practices to bring more clarity and positive emotion, such as meditation and affirmations, our minds become clear and happier, and our intuition becomes stronger. People with strong intuition are invariably happy souls as they can trust that they are guided from on high.

When we understand what intuition is as opposed to an emotion we are feeling, our life will dramatically change. We will be guided. Our higher-self will be speaking directly to us. We will know whom to speak to, when to speak to them, where to go and where not to go. This is so profoundly important for any creative person, which really means every single one of us. We will be genuinely, divinely guided. So please study this and begin with a few simple tools. Meditation practice, time and advice when followed are all that's required to help us tap into the power of our intuition.

Intuition is so beautiful, simple, and yet so profound when experienced for our spiritual growth as well as for our career and life. Intuition is the Infinite Intelligence speaking directly through us, to us!

Intuition means we are IN TUNE with God.

It doesn't matter what we choose to call God. We can call it our Magical Being, Spirit, Love, Higher-Self, or Infinite Intelligence. It doesn't matter what we choose to call it, it is our Higher Power! So, when we are awake to our intuition, we are awake and in tune with God. Duality is gone for a small amount of time and we are unified. All the knowledge and creative ideas that have ever existed are totally available to us when we take the time to stop and listen. This is great as well for writers, or anyone in life. It's so important because when we are *in tune,* our creativity flows and we don't have any blocks. *Yes, no more writer's block!*

While we are speaking of writer's block, here is a quick bit of advice to help you in your writing and creating. Profound studies and insights into how the brain operates have been made in the last few years. One of them is that it is absolutely essential to creative flow to keep the body well hydrated. Even when our body is dehydrated by only 10%, our brainpower diminishes by 30%. So, sometimes you might think you have writer's block, and you might *simply need water,* so stay hydrated.

Remember that intuition is your soul directing you to all the good and all the success in your life. Please understand creative visualization, which is sometimes referred to as guided meditation, is an excellent practice as we have mentioned, to clear the mind and our aura from all of the gunky thoughts out there. We literally become clogged. It is like ice surrounding the body and we have to melt away that ice to become clear.

Two of the most powerful ways to achieve this is to have regular physical exercise and daily meditation. Meditation helps clear the mind so that we can allow our intuition to be clearly 'heard'. In a guided visualization, we learn how to relax the mind and allow someone else to speak to us and to guide us; we start focusing on what we *do want* to manifest into our magical lives. What is also recommended after a guided visualization is simply to be still. We highly recommend any of our powerful Visualization CD's as these will help you to learn how to breathe deeply, relax and focus the mind. It is best to do this sitting up. This is especially true if you have not done any sort of visualization or guided meditation before. It takes a bit of training to quiet the mind and a visualization program is a great place to start.

Remember to inhale through your nose, hold it, and exhale slowly through your mouth. Just keep breathing. When we learn to stop thought, it feels that our higher voice is knock, knock, knocking and at last we can open the door. But if we don't slow down and become quiet, we can't hear the knocking to open the door where all of the answers are waiting to guide us to our next level of success and happiness. When we are silent, this awesome power can be heard or felt speaking to us and through us. We must learn to be still long enough so we can hear and feel our intuition. Also remember the importance of breathing, of gently focusing on our breath.

Ernest Holmes the great metaphysician who wrote *"The Science of Mind"* said, *"Intuition is not a strong emotion because when we feel emotional it is usually our old thinking."* That is such a perfect description of intuition. It is so clear. Ernest is saying that strong emotions are old paradigms. Old paradigms are our old thinking, old tapes in our mind being triggered by a situation in our human experience.

Intuition is that still, small, quiet voice. It's knowingness. So, when we have a lot of emotion involved it's usually not going to be our intuition. Emotions are not feelings. (Confused? More about that in Part Two.) Intuition doesn't seem to have any emotion and yet it does feel peaceful. It's just a thought that silently comes to us. A quiet knowingness and guidance. When we have that *knowingness* we have peace of mind and trust. It's simply beautiful. It's mystical!

A mystical experience is God speaking through us and that is also intuition. A psychic experience is all of the different thoughts that we are picking up from the collective unconscious. What is the collective unconscious? The collective unconscious holds all the thoughts and emotions from all the people in our area of the world and we tap into this cacophony of... well mainly rubbish - *and you thought all of that stuff you kept thinking about was all your own.*

How do we know if something we are thinking is really our own thought? Well this is not important, what is important is that you know whether it feels good or bad. If the thought feels bad NEXT IT!!

People become confused between the two experiences that occur in different dimensions, so let's now discuss mysticism and psychic experiences. As we just discussed, intuition is the Infinite directly speaking to us. It is a wonderful and magical power that we can all access and tap into when we pause to listen. A psychic experience is when we tap into other peoples thoughts. As a common example. You think of a friend and call them and they say they were just about to call you. We are all psychic but that is not intuition. When we use our intuition, which is our mystic connection to Spirit, now that is *real* Power. That's mysticism. You do not need another person telling you your future. YOU CREATE YOUR OWN FUTURE! Please know that you are much more powerful when you tune into the mystic part of your higher-self and not the psychic part of you, as the mystic message is directly from the Infinite, rather than that of other people's thoughts.

You are then totally one-to-one with the Infinite Intelligence, *which can never be wrong.* You don't need to go through anyone else. Remember it's all about clarity. It's so important to be clear. What's also important to know is when we are not clear, because some people *don't know* that they *don't know* and that is disempowering and somewhat sad. So, another reason why it is so important to dispel the fog, the clog from our minds, is so our consciousness will be clear, which will then allow our intuition to flow through to our conscious awareness.

When we are taking a shower, the water literally clears our aura. Aura isn't just some hippy talk. It's now proven. Neuroscientists are proving that we do have a vibrational oscillation around us and this vibration *is* in fact our aura or ethereal body. When that is blocked, nothing can flow. Ideas don't flow smoothly and we aren't able to make clear decisions. So, it's really important to use all of our own tools of the mind to become clear. We don't want to be around people who have clogged-up minds and think negatively because their advice is not to be trusted as it may be fear based. I know that when we are communicating with other people, if those around us are clear, we are not going to be manipulated by other people's fears or false judgments.

Did you know that everyone is intuitive?

It's not some great gift bestowed only upon special people. Everyone has intuitive abilities. It's just that sometimes we are clogged. We are living in a fog and we have to dispel that fog to let our intuitive powers flow through. Some people might say to someone, *"Oh, that person's really psychic."* Well, everyone's psychic. We all have a sixth sense. We can all pick up on the energies that are happening beyond the physical that is no big deal. But oh, the power of tuning in to our intuition is beautiful and can be trusted. Listen to your heart not your head. Now we know that we never need be afraid of what life has to offer if we are looking inward with spirit, because we will *know* that we are always divinely guided. All we have to do is stop and listen.

Please use your intuition. Learn to use creative visualization. Learn to be still. Learn to be on your own, turn off the TV and be still. It's really, really important to clear the mind. Get rid of the muck. Be out in nature as much as possible. When our minds are clogged and not clear we sometimes are not even consciously aware of this clogging. Anytime we are feeling fear and not experiencing true joy in our heart that is the time we know to stop, breathe and begin to do something different. Maybe go to see an uplifting movie take a walk in nature, or meditate. Have beautiful natural plants and flowers around you because they help clean your air and give you pure oxygen and good energy.

So tune into to life from within...

YOUR FREE AUDIO PROGRAM
THE SCIENCE OF BEING GREAT by
WALLACE D WATTLES

This powerful program is another FREE Gift. Read by Michele Blood with extra explanations at the end of chapters to explain the more exoteric language of that time and philosophy.

Simply type into your Internet Browser
http://www.MysticalSuccessClub.com/WallaceWattles

The Pole of Prosperity

What is The Pole Of Prosperity? It is using the Law Of Polarity and the Law of Vibration in OUR favor to create what we want into our beautiful lives. Once we love our dreams enough and then we take positive action -using the Daily Action List- then the love we have moves our actions into power actions. Love is the highest vibration there is and when we do not feel the love we can use our own minds to change our vibration so we oscillate at a faster vibration. Then our dreams are no longer wishful thinking.

Now is the time for us to learn another fast and fun method of the mind to visualize and that is *The Pole Of Prosperity.* Hermes teaching says "As above so below". Lack is actually on the same pole as prosperity, it is just the other end of the same pole. Lack is simply vibrating at a much slower frequency. Whenever we are feeling fear, anger, depression etc. we are oscillating at a slower rate, whenever we feel happy, excited and have an attitude of gratitude we are oscillating at a faster vibration. This has been proven in clinical studies and yet this was written about over four thousand years ago.

There are many actions we can take to help us powerfully manifest our hearts desire. We can help propel ourselves into great fulfilled success and take quantum leaps of increase beyond what we have ever done before. The Pole Of Prosperity is truly so simple and yet very effective. We do not do this to be ahead of the so called competition, as the vibration for thinking in a competitive way is actually thinking that there is lack and not enough to go around when in fact there is an over supply and plenty for everyone. The creative plane of life which lives over the Terror Barrier -we covered in an earlier chapter- is where all real success and change occur. Otherwise we are only using our will power and that is not enough. Our will power is important and we need this as our will power then helps us to change our old thoughts of lack *(the opposite end of the pole)* to thoughts of plenty. *(the high end of the pole)* Then, we are unifying with Infinite Universal Intelligence. This way we will get ahead of our old vibrations of *"Doing it the "hard way"* and break the spell we have considered for far too long. People say, *"Well, that's just the way it is, life is hard".* Rubbish, life is beautiful.

The Law of Polarity and The Law of Vibration

These Universal Laws show us quite simply that if there is lack in our life there is also another end to the vibration of lack and that is the vibration of prosperity. It is all a matter of using the same Pole, one end being lack and the other prosperity as mentioned. What we must do is to vibrate higher to get up the pole where prosperity lives, on high!

So use your imagination and visualize a pole with a lever at one end. See yourself moving the lever to the high end of the pole where there is unlimited prosperity, do this whenever you think about lack and feel fear embracing you. You can do this for all areas of your life: Health, Happiness, Trust, Love etc. Have a pole with a lever for each area of your life. When you do this feel your vibration - *your frequency*- going faster (higher) and then you are using The Law Of Polarity in YOUR favor. No more pendulum swing of experiences.

Your thoughts can control your vibrations by changing your lever on your pole.

Do this as many times a day as you have to. You can even physically move your arm up as if you were moving your lever to the highest end then visualize putting a lock onto this end so your levels stay high at the Prosperous High end of the pole.

Doing this will create some true magical manifestations.

There is such a beautiful prosperity and loving cycle that begins when we are in tune with higher thoughts. We are tuning our consciousness to a higher vibration using the pole of prosperity and it works so quickly. When we begin to also see that what we can achieve can also be helping others in our family and the world at large we create a bigger vision and the desire to do so becomes magnified. This also helps us tremendously to STOP our own little pity parties, which can only lead to self-destructive thinking and behaviors, which is at the opposite end of the pole where the lever is hardly moved.

We deserve to achieve all we can and we deserve to allow ourselves to be the VERY best we can be. Let us set forth the intention of making our own lives BIGGER, to increase more, increase more in abundance, in success and create an increase of more spiritual awareness.

If this still does not make sense to you lets do this simple exercise. See a volume control fader that is similar to what you find in a recording studio. You move the fader up and the volume goes up. So right now where do you see the fader leveled at with your present financial consciousness? Is it right at the bottom or mid way up? Get the picture now?

So where you see the fader imagine yourself moving it up. It is a simple exercise but it really does change your vibration in relation to money. Move that pole up as many times a day as you wish. You can even actually move your arm up as you do this/ and yell out.

I AM AT THE TOP OF THE PROSPERITY POLE YIPEEE!!

Perhaps your neighbors will simply think you are exercising or that you have won the lottery. So think big and get clear on your goals and move your lever at the high end of your pole and keep it there. Have fun with this exercise. Simple, fast, fun and it works.

So friends this is the end of this book but the beginning of your new life. For those who wish to study further you can now move ahead to Part Two and ENTER THE SEA OF UNLIMITED CONSCIOUSNESS...

One more thing... Before you go onto Part Two, we have added a new life affirmation script. Just add in your own name and career position. Change the words, add your own words. This is simply a guide as an example to show you how to write a new life script.

Put more fun in your funds and Be A Magnet To All Good

Thank yourself for reading. Believe in yourself for you are an unlimited spiritual POWERHOUSE!

And one more thing... remember to smile ☺

To Book Bob Proctor for your next event go to www.BobProctor.com
Get his amazing best selling book
"You Were Born Rich"
and his other powerful book
"Its Not About The Money"

To Book Michele Blood for your next event go to www.MicheleBlood.com

My New Life

I _____am now so grateful and happy with my wealthy, prosperous, creative, successful, joy-filled, passionate, healthy, aware magical life!

I am now open and available to receive more good than ever before and I am allowing my Higher Power to express through me as increased awareness, money, supply, love, enthusiasm and success. I am now working doing what I absolutely love to do as a _____and I am earning a great increase in profitable money doing what I love to do.

Positive opportunities and wonderful work continues to come to me every day as I take positive action. I rehearse before hand in my mind the way I want my life to be. All involved including myself have profited greatly and continue to profit greatly with all of the new opportunities. All of this and even greater good is happening in my life every moment! I am now irresistible to my huge success. I focus in the NOW so that I AM in Empowered States at all times!! I am literally A Magnet To Money, Success, Positive Opportunities, Divine Ideas and Support as It is all within me. I also have extra money come to me every week in totally unexpected right ways. Every day I expect and accept profitable surprises.

I am so thankful to my Higher Power for moving me today to a higher consciousness, in Divine Oneness, so that God's Kingdom is revealed to me and all in my experience is happy, protected, richly rewarding and successful. I am useful to my creator and to this world.

So much love and thanks,

_____
(sign your full name)

Enter The Sea Of Unlimited Consciousness

By
Michele Blood

Dedication and Thanks

Part Two is dedicated to John Endara, and friends J'en El, Dr. Lawrence T. Bond, & Treavor Rogers. You have always seen the Light and intention in our loving work and your unwavering faith has been a rock. Words could never express my respect, gratitude and love. You are a light to me and all who know you.

I would also like to express my deepest gratitude to all the Enlightened Ones who have supported and taught me and countless others: Ms Nicole Grace, Sri Ramakrishna, Jesus The Christ, Rama, Lord Buddha, Swami Muktananda, Joel S. Goldsmith, Paramahansa Yogananda, Guruji and The Holy Light of Eternity which is always present.

The Sea Of Unlimited Consciousness

Why do we create so many dramas into our lives? We do it at an unconscious level so that we can create energy. Strong emotions, even if they are emotions of anger, do create energy and with this energy we feel alive! Creating energy through anger or drama does not last very long and depletes us of even more energy after the initial rush. There are many other ways to create power and positive energy. If you wish to stop this repetitive life filled with drama please read this part of the book with an open mind. If some of it sounds too esoteric do not be concerned for your soul is getting it at a cellular level.

I too have created dramas to feel alive but no more. My awakening began in 1989. I am lying in a hospital bed after a near fatal car accident. The doctors are telling me of my many internal injuries and what lay ahead of me in terms of long, major operations and physical limitations I will have to live with. It was not a good prognosis as far as they were concerned. But little did they or I know at the time what truly was ahead of me.

People have asked when I am going to write about the true adventures of my life from rock singer to what I am now doing as it is a pretty entertaining story that even to me sounds like spiritual science-fiction. Maybe I will write all the details of my life experiences one day, however for now what is most important to me is you and how these experiences can assist you in your awakening.

In this section of the book we will be speaking about meditation practices and what true awaking is all about which can take you, as it has me and others, to lands and mystical experiences and such success and happiness you could never presently dream are possible. Oh, my friend reading this book right now, please know that absolutely everything is possible for you. There are zero limitations once we are connected to eternity. Now I know that there are no accidents in life and that my car 'accident' was the beginning of a new life into an adventure beyond my wildest imaginings. The awakening of consciousness. Do I now have any physical limitations? No. Indeed I am healthy and more alive today than ever I was in my twenties. There are no limitations, only what we accept in our mind. Was it worth all the physical pain and many months in the hospital? OH yes.

Now what has this to do with this Sea Of Unlimited Consciousness or Prosperity? Everything! For my awakening to consciousness set me on a path where my background as a rock singer/songwriter would bring to the world music to assist in serving others to wake up to their own unlimited consciousness. That is how my journey into 'real life' and MusiVation™ began. Little did I know as I was in excruciating pain in that hospital bed that this little rock singer from Sydney, Australia would travel the world and share the stage with many amazing speakers like Bob Proctor, Dr Deepak Chopra, Dr Wayne Dyer, and so many others and speak to corporations and groups all over the world. In other words if I can have this kind of a miraculous life ANYONE can!

I have been highly blessed indeed to meet Teachers of Light that may not be world-renowned, but are none the less changing this world's future to a brighter one through their highly evolved states of consciousness. In fact without Enlightenment we would all be lost. There is so much more going on behind the scene that is truly Amazing Grace and it is Pure Consciousness!

That word again and again, consciousness...Well in this section of the book we are going to delve deeper into the meaning of this word. Pure consciousness is our God self. When some say they are aware, awake etc. what they are saying is, they are consciously aware and one with their God self and I do not mean their brain. I mean one with

Omnipresent, Omniscient, and Omnipotent God/Good. When we become more and more one with pure consciousness we are set free spiritually. Free from what? Free from our belief in bondage to person, place, thing or circumstance. We 'think' - when we are at a Level One or the human state of mind that outside conditions or luck are running our lives and are the cause of our happiness, relationships, careers, sorrow, lack or prosperity.

What are the secrets to living in higher states of consciousness? Eastern philosophy has been teaching these so called secrets of higher consciousness for thousands of years so there is no real secret here. What we have here is the great mystery of consciousness. This mystery is something we must discover in our own Sea Of Unlimited Consciousness.

There are many thousands of Levels of awareness we go through as we begin to become free so we are not to judge where we are now, but to know that it is indeed not only possible to be free but that it CAN indeed happen. If you desire this so called prosperity consciousness to have material freedom, great, but there is far more to it than just using the law of attraction.

There are many laws in Eternity. The law of attraction can, if we do not delve deeper, keep us stuck in human mind or Level Two at best. If we really desire with all of our being to be free and stop the ridiculous, insane repetition of experiences we do not want, we MUST learn how to tune into pure consciousness. THERE ARE NO LIMITATIONS in pure consciousness. There is peace, love, prosperity, joy and bliss beyond comprehension. Whether we believe this or not does not stop it from being true.

However we have to start somewhere to Enter The Sea Of Unlimited Consciousness, so let us begin today by living in this moment. Doing all things, even making a cup of tea, with our full attention and gratitude. Right now new energies are here waking us up so we must be prepared spiritually for all these changes that are happening quickly on our beautiful planet. The 2nd part of this book gives some guidance to all you may be feeling as you rise higher into oneness of Divine consciousness.

There is a secret that is beyond and can lead to the mystery of all that is ...It is Pure Consciousness.

Welcome to The Sea Of Unlimited Consciousness where the beauty, abundance and love is breathtaking...

Levels into The Sea Of Unlimited Consciousness

If you wish to become, as Paramahansa Yogananda said, 'A Smile Millionaire', then this part of the book will be of great interest to you. When we can learn how to free ourselves from the sorrows of this world then true happiness and supply always follows. Plus this sort of wealth and happiness continuously flows. So as you are reading this book open your mind to what is possible and SMILE!

So now let us go into the Sea of Eternity. We are already one with the Sea Of Eternity but we have become a block of ice and do not realize that all we have to do is melt this ice to become consciously one again. Meditation practice and other mindful actions that we have already touched in part one, will free us; will melt the ice that is coating our true self. The ice is our current belief in a word of multiplicity or duality. This Sea of Eternity is deep and unfathomable and so is our true self; we all live in this Sea of Unlimited Consciousness. Some are simply paddling, too tentative to go deeper so stay in the shallow shores not yet ready to take the plunge into deeper waters. Some are braver and wade in up to their hearts. Some swim into the deep, while others dive as mermaids and others ARE the Sea itself. Most of the world are convinced that there is a Divine Power of some description operating in our human lives; but most are not sure what this power is, and do not know how to bring the Divine Presence into their daily lives and experience. If you wish to melt the ice, please read on with an open heart and mind. Freedom from lack and/or sorrow will be your Divine reward.

Freedom, peace and prosperity are not dependent on circumstances, people or conditions. We have covered this quite thoroughly in Part One "Become A Magnet To Money" you have just read. But if you wish to truly *free your soul* so that you can swim into the depths of the Infinite Sea than Part Two in this volume on consciousness will, I pray, illuminate you to *'see'* the possibilities, that is the intention. This is a much deeper conversation. When we reach the depth of our soul, and allow IT to take over our life experience, a peace, confidence and serenity that we could never have dreamed possible *can* be realized. *Freedom* from the world's sorrows is our soul's purpose and freedom from our own sorrow will serve others. This *freedom* from the veil of illusion is... **God's Grace.**

After completing the first part "Become A Magnet To Money" I realized that there may still be many questions unanswered. This section of the book is for those who *do* desire to go beyond Level Two and experience REAL FREEDOM. Sometimes we can get stuck in *the getting of stuff* so here we have deeper insights into what and how we manifest or gain conscious awareness so that we can live in The Sea Of Unlimited Consciousness, consciously. It is possible! The intention here is for you to understand with more clarity the beauty of consciousness and hence decide for yourself whether you wish to further your studies by these spiritual contemplations and ideas. It is suggested that you go back and read Part One again after you have read Part Two. You may be surprised to notice how much more you will understand. Understanding consciousness helps release our ignorance as ignorance simply leads to fear. Here is an oldie but a goodie...

F E A R: False-Evidence-Appearing-Real

It is with deep love and positive light filled intention that these ideas will assist you to more fully realize the magnificence of your soul as you grow in loving awareness about your spiritual consciousness. YES, we desire to live better, wealthier, fuller lives. However we do not wish to get stuck *in the getting of stuff*, which is not what this journey is about. It is about *consciousness;* it is about unity with our Soul. Here we will cover some of the different experiences that we go through and what we are calling Levels into...**The Sea of Unlimited Consciousness...**

Please do your best to not judge where you are now swimming or at what Level your friends are presently swimming as we go back and forth quite a bit on this journey. This will simply give you more clarity about these Levels. Do your best to open your heart and absorb these words. There are thousands of mind states in and during all of these Levels; however I am not attempting to discuss all of these many mind states here. For this conversation, let's keep it simple and again use the KISS technique.

K I S S: Keep-It-Simple-and-Spiritual

I Love what Shakespeare wrote: "*All the world's a stage, and all the men and women merely players; they have their exits and their entrances,*" - from "As You Like It." Which part are we now playing? That is the question... We are acting a different role, on and in, each stage or Level. These Levels are the different stages we experience in spiritual awareness; simply a new conscious awareness that we experience when we start asking questions and begin to study and desire to discover what this thing called life is and who we really are! *Who am I pretending to be today? Who am I really? Am I a good swimmer or still splashing at the shore?* So what Level of awareness we are presently experiencing is not really the point. The point is to know that there is much more to discover. As Bob and I covered in the first part of the book visualize what you want not what you don't want. I did not realize I had always used visualization and rehearsed not just with my band but with my life. I rehearesed in my mind the way I wished things to be. Little did I realize how much this positive way of looking at my life would affect my future.

When we begin to have even a small understanding of these Levels we can begin to recognize: *Oh I see, that is where I am now swimming.* Or, to note when we did only paddle at the shore of awareness and now feel the freedom of being able to swim, can be so freeing. Contemplation is what it is about. Going deeper and beyond...

We perhaps have long discarded the fear of swimming through the waves to deeper clearer waters and have left our paddling friends far behind us. We may turn around sometimes to wave back at them but they cannot see us over the Sea's ocean waves, so we bid them *adieu* from our heart and swim on. Which is what we must sometimes do, if we truly desire to grow and wake up!

It is empowering to be a strong swimmer and to know that if needed, we can rescue those who attempted to swim out and got caught in the tides. It is also vital to know our own strength and if we are not strong enough swimmers at this present moment to *not* do rescue work as then we could both be in danger of drowning in the rip tides, or at the least being swept back to shore. *Phew... Oh that's where I was. Now I know to simply let go when caught in the tides and I will soon be in safe calm water. I got through those rip tides, wow!*

This can really give us clarity to know that we are in fact moving forward even when appearances on the outside do not as yet seem to have changed. The change is happening within. We are raising our vibration; we are actually making progress and learning how to swim. Often times what happens is we allow the appearance of what we are experiencing *now* to dictate what Level we are at and that is NOT always the truth. We could be oscillating much faster/higher than we are humanly aware of, and through *a dark night of the soul* experience or ignorance go back to the shoreline of the same old experiences. For heavens sake, and I do mean for HEAVENS SAKE let us

PLEASE ignore the present appearances good or bad and let's swim deeper...

Spiritual insights and experiences cannot be discerned through the intellect; however insights may unfold in our conscious awareness as a result of understanding thoughts received *through* the intellect. Knowing something is not simply remembering information. True *knowing* is spiritual awareness and discernment. Spirit is unfolding and experiencing *for us* through our awareness. So if you have been reading any of this book and have said to yourself: *Well I know that, this is all old information to me.* STOP and ask yourself: *But do I really know or is it simply information I have stored in my memory? Do I really know or am I still experiencing the same old stuff?* Be honest with yourself. These questions and ideas are not to hold judgment against ourselves, but are here to help us grow and help us to absorb ourselves in Spirit. So for heavens sake, let's breathe, let go, relax and let our soul do the knowing for us! Let's surrender to Omniscience!

The way to really *know* is through our feeling nature or intuition - which is not our emotions nor is it our intellect, it is our consciousness. There could be a time where we think we are progressing and then we feel stuck, still on the same shoreline or stage of life, and this can be quite painful and frustrating. This happens often when we do not see appearances externally changing as I have now mentioned numerous times. This can also happen because things are going great and we become lazy with our spiritual practices. Without realizing we have disconnected to our source. I wish for you to really GET this and to not judge by appearances good or bad, as that will only keep you stuck and frustrated. In that emotion of frustration we can stop progressing deeper into the Sea. The emotional fears can actually slow us down from progressing because we have allowed our present experiences to dictate where we are, instead of our spiritual awareness or feeling nature. At other times we do not realize we are growing in awareness however we may be growing and are not aware of it with our intellect; our intellect can be a trickster at times and can attempt to make us *think* it knows better than our spiritual consciousness.

A person may swim deeper into the Sea of Unlimited Consciousness simply by being mindful with their work and attitude and holding onto their dreams with focus and positive, enthusiastic action. A person who can live in the now and stay focused has a far greater opportunity to raise their awareness without realizing at the time what is happening. In actuality you may *think* someone is at the shoreline but they may be in fact swimming far into this magical Eternal Sea.

When we are not fully awake and still have our consciousness clogged, we have no way of discerning the vibrations in others; there are sometimes obvious hints we can be aware of with individuals of high consciousness. They will not be reactive to outside conditions and will seem almost at times Pollyannaish in their enthusiasm for life and all its possibilities...almost childlike. They will have a peaceful, happy vibration and will always be ready for the next adventure. They will have a youthful radiance about them irrespective of their human age. They will be persistent in their dreams no matter what and the word risk will not be in their vocabulary. Every creative endeavor will be completed no matter what. They never give up and when they make decisions they stick to them. These people could be scientists, musicians or even the local video store guy. They will do each job or project with love and focus. They do not brag nor do anything to make it all about them. You feel happier when with them and more hopeful about everything! They really listen.

Even if they are flamboyant and outgoing in personality you will never really know who they are because they will always shift the attention in conversation onto something else or back to you. They will give you some personal information but only enough to satisfy any curiosities you have about their lives. They will do this so tactfully and beautifully that you will not even think they are being mysterious. Of course their close friends know more about them but with acquaintances they do not share too much information. What we do know is we simply feel good when we are in their company. So I will repeat again and again throughout this conversation, we can NEVER judge just WHO is standing right in front of us. When our vibration is rising, things will begin shifting for the better. We are happier, less stressed, more peaceful and things start showing up that we have wanted i.e. romance, companionship; prosperity increases, business opportunities are coming to us from out of the blue, unique ideas are flowing, etc. All of a sudden we realize: *Wow, I don't argue with people anymore and they don't argue with me. I am really happy. Gee, everyone around me is smiling. Even the flowers are smiling*!

So now let's go back to the beginning, to the shoreline-paddlers (or Level One). When we begin to shift in awareness and notice that good things are happening to us we are coming into the heart, or slightly deeper Sea depths or Level Two. Now we are prepared to go deeper with the following information and spiritual ideas. In the reading and digesting of these words allow new spiritual illumination and spiritual absorption to be experienced.

A transmission of light-awareness so to speak may be realized and experienced if you are open to it. It is a Divine Current that enters our brain and can be actually felt as tingling. This current illuminates the parts of the brain that hold old negative habits of belief and purifies our thoughts. We begin to not only attract more good we also begin to be only attracted to that which is for our Highest Good and the Highest Good for all. It is a mystery and it is beautiful. God's gift of Grace! It is challenging, as mentioned, to find words to explain to the intellect what

cannot be explained. Most of us do require exoteric*
teachings to experience the real teachings which are
esoteric#.

These experiences allow our souls to download
awareness through our feeling/knowing nature. So please
surrender some of your old beliefs and intellect and smile
this is *NOT serious.* This is joyous and beautiful! If we all
knew how deeply loved we are, we would be overpowered
with tears of bliss and gratitude. We are Pure Spirit, One
with Eternity. Light is being transmitted to each and every
one of us *all* of the time but most are too clogged by the
world's ideas and thoughts to feel it.

May these words of love, assist your Light to be felt
so you can be on purpose and experience who you really
are! We are *powerful, beautiful spiritual beings* simply
having a physical experience. We are not doing this
alone. We are never, ever alone. But it is NOT this book
nor the words that will ultimately serve you, it is your
very own consciousness. It may not be felt or realized
today but somewhere down the track of life there could
be a HUGE AHA!!

Welcome, for we are now entering **The Sea Of Unlimited Consciousness into Level One...**

---

* Exoteric knowledge is ascertained by the intellect.
\# Esoteric inner, knowing. A direct realization into consciousness.

Level One
The human experience

So let's talk about the First Level to the Sea of Unlimited Consciousness...The human experience. At this Level we are paddling at the shores of the Sea. We are not aware of a higher power other than what we have been taught to believe in church or school. Some of us may feel Spirit abundantly when we are very young and then the world's density of matter (*Maya*) educates and clogs up our true self, which is pure consciousness, out of our awareness. We are *grown up* now and do not wish to delve into such silliness as we are living in the '*real world'*.

At this Level we do not truly feel nor think of God, Soul, etc. We may *think* we believe in a higher power but never truly contemplate with our busy lives what 'It' really is. We may go to church however we usually go out of habit, or, fear of what others think of us. Not for the true love of God in us. We think we love God and our church, and we may react strongly if anyone else does not hold our same beliefs. These strong reactions come from fear not love. We are mostly concerned with ourselves and our human experience; who is doing what to whom and who agrees with us is of paramount importance. Some say they have faith and then when someone debates if a God even exists they get up on their high horse and become very angry. WHY? If we had true faith we would not react at all. True faith never needs to stick up for itself and does not react. Let others live their own life. Debating is what starts wars and corrupts innocence.

Many never get past this first Level and stand on the safe shoreline and that is fine, we are not here to judge simply to have a deeper look into our own soul. I love what Wallace D. Wattles wrote in "The Science Of Being Great" he said: "*All is right with the world. It is perfect and advancing to completion. All men and women everywhere are good and perfect. We are in the process of becoming."*

Yes, we are in the process of becoming. This is a beautiful way of looking at each other and our world as opposed to looking for what is wrong. We are in the process of becoming. Most at Level One are judgmental and reactionary and find it much easier simply to blame the world for what is wrong in their lives rather than looking within. *They did it to me. It was because of so and so. That happened because the bus was late, it was not in my control, it wasn't my fault, etc.*

At this Level we think what happens in our experience is mostly out of our control and we do not like having to take responsibility for our experiences, good or bad. We are not aware that we co-create our own world. At this Level we usually have no deep thought as to how our experiences come to be. We think that luck, hard work, persistence or perhaps even destiny creates our reality, good or bad. Yes we make *some* things happen through will power and hard work but beyond that we are lost as to what is really going on behind the scenes, so to speak, in our thoughts and beliefs. Will power is important but when we delve deeper and combine it with Divine Will Power than... WOW!!

There have been many talented and very intelligent people who are outdone in success time and time again by others of a far less talent. We may wonder why they make it and not ourselves when we think we are obviously way superior in talent or intellect to them. Our speculations do not, at this Level, look within. We say they are just lucky or knew someone or had good timing. *How did they get to know someone? Why do they have such good timing?* These are much better questions to contemplate. There is great power in questions. We do not realize that the inner power or consciousness of these so called *lucky* people was what assisted them in achieving success where we had failed. They could also have a lot of empowerment from past lives that is positively affecting this life. But we will go into that deeper conversation further on.

At Level One we think all that is happening in our lives is being dictated by outside forces; people, places or circumstances. And when someone say at a Level Two comes in desiring to help a Level One person by claiming that they can change their own lives and create their own reality, the person at Level One will look at this person and in all honest sincerity exclaim, *You simply do not understand, it was out of my control, I had no choice. You just don't understand the circumstances, etc.* Better swim out of there fast or the rip tide - if you are not as yet a Level Three or Four swimmer, will take you both down and back to the shore...

We may seem quite happy people on the surface at Level One, but if we delve deeper we may find a victim mentality raising its face in our very own mirror when no one else is looking. No matter what someone says to us, at this Level we truly believe it's all outside forces creating our experience; it's the boyfriend who just doesn't get it, the boss, or my parents. The list goes on. It is never, ever us. We find the same old boyfriend, job, etc., all with different names and guises and the same old experiences are created again and again. We never wonder *why?*

All we do at this Level is say we are unlucky in love or at work or whatever it is - blah, blah, blah, and justify this, justify that. Phew...Reaction, reaction, reaction. *It's my father's fault, it's my mother's fault, it's my teacher's fault, it's the guy I was married to, these people are evil, etc.* There is good luck, bad luck, good people, bad people, there's prosperity, there's lack, there's good timing, there's bad timing. There's everything else controlling our life. Our shoreline buddies will endorse everything we say, because if they do not agree with us then they too may have to start taking responsibility for their own lives, and goodness knows we do not want that!

So this is the merry go round of the human experience. "Ground Hog Day" over and over again. (Check out this insightful and quite mystical movie!) At this Level we have to believe in good and bad. Do not judge but simply observe how some prosperous nations live at Level One and play the litigation game, taking people to court left right and center as if it were all a game, instead of working things out through love and open hearted communication. We do not realize as yet that what we do to another we do to ourselves and we wonder why we are not happier. It's an interesting role we play at this Level, yes indeed a very interesting sleep walking experience. I will repeat again and again...observe, however DO NOT judge. It is a human experience simply evolving, as Wallace D. Wattles said. *"We are in the process of becoming."*

Even when we think we come from a kind heart, when we are at the shorelines we may still persist in our good natured claims, with, *Oh, that person, I do feel sorry for them and the way they treat me is simply because they just don't realize what a good person I am. How silly and ignorant they are to be missing out on this much love. All I want to do is love them. Oh well I guess there are just ignorant people in the world.* And then we judge by justification that a person is bad, wrong or dumb if they do not like us or want to date us or work with us. We react, judge or shutdown to stop feeling any pain. But the pain will come up and raise its head in some other way.

This is all another way to stay stuck. So even if we come from what we *think* is a good attitude, there's still a little judgment going on. *We are correct and they are...well perhaps a little off balance to not like or appreciate such a good loving person and it is their loss.* We are the ones who feel pain with this sort of attitude but don't wish to admit it. This does not help, it is only a band aid and the pain plus anger will come later and may be taken out on an innocent bystander. Better off admitting we feel hurt and forgive ourselves and move on. How? By living in the moment not in the past nor in the future. Confused? Keep reading...

We may even justify hurt feelings by thinking we are higher in evolution because we *think we* believe in God and have a happier attitude, but if we are still judging and being reactionary, then at the shorelines we will remain or at the very least up to our knees in the shallows. We may want to wade out into the deeper waters but the water is still too murky or too cold, we exclaim, to go swimming today!

They, just don't get me, I am spiritual you know. This was simply a lesson. Can't you see that my back is sore because I've got weight on my shoulders right now and...? We may oscillate between Level One and Level Two with these types of thoughts. We hold a lot of judgments and false ideas when we first start practicing the law of attraction and metaphysics. And we *know it all*. We have all the language down and all the terminology. And we can be up there on our soap boxes and tell you exactly what's wrong with you. We've all gone through these mind states so we can laugh at ourselves and think, *I can't believe I used to do that!* But we are evolving. *Perfect but not yet complete* and it's all necessary for most of us to experience; if we can but recognize it within ourselves it may stop us from judging others.

Let us now go into Level Two of this Miraculous, Magical Sea...

Level Two
I am more than my body

Level Two is so exciting and fun. Here is where we are melting the ice of duality and our Light is beginning to shine through the ice. We now awaken to the idea that there is more to this human experience than meets the eye. Our vibration is oscillating at a faster speed and this vibration heats and melts the ice. We now begin to wake up. Even if at first this has just been through the intellect questioning what life is *really* all about. A feeling of spiritual awareness has been sparked that we do indeed co-create our own reality. We have begun to be more *mindful* and *contemplative.* This is indeed a powerful time, so let us now discuss how we can raise our awareness even further.

Being mindful helps tremendously to melt the ice of ignorance. So how do we practice being *mindful* and what is it? Mindfulness is to be happy in the here and now, in the moment. Focusing on this moment. Keeping our mind on what we are doing in every moment. Seeing the beauty of all things. Being positive and happy in the moment. This is not easy, to be mindful in each moment, but it is vital if we wish to grow in awareness. Use the MusiVation™ music and the other tools we discussed in Part One, as these tools assist beautifully with being mindful because at this Level mindfulness is vital for our progress into deeper Levels. It is just in the higher Levels we do not need the tools, per say, as much. Our mind and heart connection to our soul is the POWER!

At Level Two we begin to study the universal laws of attraction and polarity and do our best as mentioned to be *mindful.* We are waking up to the idea that we are more than our bodies and we are going deeper into the Sea of self discovery. We start to feel Divine Awareness within us. A spark has come alive. We begin to study, ask questions, and look within to our Spirit for the answers to life's questions. We begin to have such a thirst to know more about our spirit and desire deeply to better understand what is *really* going on through our conscious awareness.

How did we wake up to be experiencing this Level Two of awareness?

This is different for every soul and there are many deep answers to this mystery. But at this stage a mystery it remains even though present appearances attempt to tell us a different story. Only our soul has the true answer as this involves what personal power and awareness we brought to this life from other lives and so much more in-depth ideas that for now further explanation may only cause confusion and too much intellectualizing.

Suffice it to say the spark can be turned on by any number of experiences: It may be this very book you are now reading; a sign post; watching a film; a feeling of being soul sick and deciding that the love we have been searching for in others is actually right where we are. It could be from a physical or emotional shock like losing a lover or friend.

My second wake up call to Spirit was through a car accident in 1989. But let me go back a bit. I was actually born in a small outback town in NSW. I would sing all the time with no shyness from the age of 1 and 1/2 but I did not really talk much just sang as I could feel people became happy when I sang. Then my family moved to the Blue Mountains, again a very small town and I attended a catholic school and here was my first wake up as I fell in love, yes at age 4 I fell in love with God and any person who talked about God was the best person in the world to me. I adored ALL the nuns, Jesus, any saint I read about and I would beg to go to mass every morning to be with these wonderful happy Irish nuns. It got to a point that when my family where leaving to go to Sydney to live and the nuns tried to persuade my mother, who was not a Catholic, to live with them for the rest of the year. Mum, said a large NO, as she did not want me, her young daughter now only 9, eventually becoming a nun. All I know is I wept and wept to leave my beloved nuns who I felt deeply knew what I was feeling.

I went on to become a Pop Singer and toured all over Australia 49 weeks a year.

Then in 1989 I had a near fatal car accident. My love for the Divine woke up in me again powerfully. I prayed and sang for my own healing and I was healed and then Dr Wayne Dyer, Dr Deepak Chopra, Bob Proctor and Stuart Wilde said after touring with me, that what I had was magical and could reach many peoples lives and so encouraged me to tour the world. I did this living in Malaysia and then coming to the USA. However I was during that time really searching for truth. I went to 34 countries and I never found anyone who was truly in love with God who could teach me. My love was becoming so intense and so was my search. I went to the United States and started doing my work and music and began doing prayer recordings for others, as I am always guided to do what I have to do, I never question it and found peoples lives were transforming but I still had to find a REAL TEACHER.

In 2006 I finally met with true Enlightenment and at last had found a TRUE ENLIGHTENED TEACHER. Two years later after intense study and meditation I also went to my next level of evolution and it continues to transform me every day and I am now again praying for others and life is overflowing with Light and Happiness.
(For Prayer requests go to www.MysticalSuccessClub.com)

Now let's get back to Level Two of awareness, which can be a very challenging and yet a spiritually adventurous time in our lives as we circumnavigate what this world of Spirit has to offer. It can be very fulfilling, joy filled and rewarding as we begin to read every spiritual, new thought and mystical book we can get our hands on. We go on a quest for Truth and read many books, study new thought, astrology, mysticism, metaphysics, and so forth. We may go to churches or to different teachers and feel a deep fascination in subjects that never before held any interest. In fact at Level One we would have found them outright boring and so 'out there'. Now we want to know what our purpose is. We now feel we are truly swimming in the depths of the Sea. It is wonderful!

And to note here: If you began your search because of wanting more money and being sick and tired of your old way of living that is fine. We must all desire to have richer more fulfilling lives. It is our Divine Birthright. It does not matter what triggers us to become seekers of Truth! As long as it is not wishful thinking about becoming wealthier or changing your life. This Level is not about wishful thinking, this is about change and decision. Deciding we ARE going to have a better life and then going for it!!

We begin at Level Two to ask many questions. *What is my purpose? There's got to be more than this, what more can I do?* We also begin to open our hearts to other's pain and look for ways we can be of service. We begin to see our world and others in a whole new Light!! Our Divine Spark has been ignited and we feel joyous and confident. We begin to meet other like minded souls who are also swimming into deeper waters. We are not alone on our quest. How marvelous! We realize that life is truly magical!

We study affirmative prayer and think positive thoughts about what we *can* do. We may also begin to enjoy manifesting *stuff* through visualization practices. We are determined to clear away the quagmire that had us mesmerized and to take charge of our life's experience. Some may begin to meditate at Level Two, however real love and enjoyment of meditation does not seem to come to full appreciation until Level Three. Most of us are more interested in clearing away old habits and in learning how to use the law of attraction in our favor than in meditation practices. Which is fine...we do what we have to do at whatever Level of awareness we are now experiencing. We all go through it. (Except for rare high beings. More about that later) We are ready when we are ready, it is as simple as that!

For some the main focus and why we begin these studies and practices could be to heal our bodies, clear emotional issues or to begin attracting money and success. *Hey there Michele, wait a minute,* you may exclaim, *that is the reason I purchased this book, to Become A Magnet To Money.*

Was it? WAS IT? Is it perhaps FREEDOM you want?

There are no coincidences in life - you are still reading because you want to know more, so please be patient and keep reading... and smile!

Of course every one of us has every right to want to enjoy the good things in life and if we really swim into deeper waters we may find that what we really desire is FREEDOM! And yes money can serve to live life more freely so it is good and right to desire money. There is absolutely nothing wrong in desiring more of the good things in life, we have every Divine right to do so. It is in fact our Divine heritage. We are the beloved offspring of The Divine Presence and the Kingdom of God is ours. Feel better now?

We have to have *some* sort of incentive to keep up our spiritual studies and practices at this Level and good health, love, and yes good old fashioned money is as good an incentive as anything else at this Level of our growth. The affirmations and visualization exercises we practice at this Level are powerful and positive and do serve as great tools to melt away some of the collective thoughts and mesmerizing affects we have taken on during this lifetime. We live with over *six billion* other souls on this planet so of course we are going to take on other people's thoughts and impressions.

The MusiVation™ positive affirmation songs and visualization programs help us tremendously at this Level to clear away old negative beliefs we have held for so long. At the very least we will have a more positive outlook on life and become happier and more enthusiastic and have a few more bucks in the bank. Nothing wrong with that! We can also become more successful as most people are magnetically drawn to happy people who have a *we can do it* attitude. This is why some people who we feel to be less talented than we are, get the best gigs, happy relationships and better situations in life because of their positive attitude. At Level One we are stumped as to why, it seems so unfair. We could not comprehend this before but now we know that most people love a happy, positive, giving person to work with or befriend whether they admit to it or not. A happy person is an *attract*-ive person!

I always love to use the example from films, as many films that have been created, show us how to swim in the Sea! I have a feeling that if Jesus the Christ was born in today's world he may have been a film maker as he was a great story teller. He knew that people learn best from hearing a story. With a story we are less likely to take it personally or become reactive. We are being entertained and have our whole attention focused.

One movie, as an example of waking up from Level One to Two is "The Truman Show" with Jim Carrey. Jim played the part of Truman Burbank. Truman is a man whose life is a fake. The place he lives is in fact a big studio lot with hidden cameras everywhere, and all his friends and people around him are actors who play their roles in the most popular TV show in the world, "The Truman Show." Truman thinks that he is an ordinary but happy man with an ordinary life and has no idea about how he is being exploited. After being married a few years he felt the itch to leave his home town and explore, go on vacation somewhere exotic but he was always thwarted from leaving. There were always perfectly logical and legitimate excuses given from the people (actors) in his town that stopped him from leaving.

Truman started feeling very suspicious and uncomfortable, even in his own home. He was beginning to swim into deeper waters and waking up into Level Two where he knew there must be more to life than this. He started realizing, *This isn't normal. How come that bike keeps on going around at the same time?* He started noticing things and he felt very suspicious. He did find one person who tried to tell him the truth, a beautiful girl he was falling in love with who suddenly disappeared from his town. But he still had to risk his life sailing across what he thought was a dangerous ocean during a violent storm to discover he was on a Huge TV sound stage and his whole life had been a set up, a lie... Sound familiar?

What a great metaphor for life! Now again I am going to remind us all: there is no better or worse Level in this thing called life, it simply *is.* I know I have said *bad* or *good* experiences earlier, but this is simply a way to attempt to explain with mere words. So please do your best to not be too hard on yourself nor to judge others, we at this Level do not know where someone else is at in The Sea of Unlimited Consciousness. We have no clue sometimes to just whom is standing right in front of us. Attempting to judge others is useless and actually can take us backwards to the shore as our ego has become too involved. The ego loves for us to judge as then we do not feel *less than*. Only the Divine Presence within truly knows. It is only this world that judges. What was right or wrong one hundred years or even fifty years ago is now laughed at as antiquated thinking.

Now in Level Two, we are at last aware enough to recognize when negative judgment rears its ugly head, *oh wow, I've got to say next and stop this negative judging of myself or others. Only joyful grateful thoughts and feelings belong with me now. This is just old stinking thinking; they're not my true thoughts or feelings. That's the human experience. That isn't where love lives.*

Now watch out people, for here we are at Level Two and we now have a little spiritual knowledge of the universal laws and fancy ourselves as somewhat experts on spiritual and metaphysical matters. We go about and let everyone know just why they are creating this or that bad experience into their life. Even when no one has asked our advice, and without even a moments hesitation, we begin to share all the reasons why a person is not in happier or in more fortunate circumstances. So if we have been guilty of such an act let us now forgive ourselves and move on. We were, we thought, at the time only wishing to be of service.

It is best at this Level to only give advice when asked or simply BE the example by demonstrating a good life. We do not know why someone is having a certain experience. It may be to wake them up to a higher Level of success and purpose. Most of us go through this at one time or another at this Level, I most certainly did. As mentioned we never know where another truly is within their own consciousness and they may simply be requiring certain life experiences to assist them in waking up, or they may be a Level Three or Four and are simply showing the world a different face so as to be anonymous to who they truly are. We realize at these Levels that most people would not understand and would in fact think we were crazy if we shared what we really know to be true, so we are quiet unless we feel the person is ready to hear. Why set ourselves up to ridicule or debate! We have nothing to stand up for or defend we simply know it and live it. We are simply doing our best to be clear vehicles for God's Grace...but more about that further on.

Many of us have experienced seeing ourselves judging others. I have seen the most wonderful souls judged negatively when people had NO IDEA who they truly were. Some of these souls were great teachers but because of an old paradigm we seem to come with a ready made image of what a teacher on the spiritual path should look like, live and how they should be in the world. If this person acts in any way off what we have been programmed to think a spiritual teacher should act or be we *should* all over them. *Do not let appearances fool you.* Many teachers of Light and even Enlightened Masters were and are quite outrageous in their personalities and this is because certain outrageous comments are necessary when teaching to assist certain individuals to wake up and swim off the shoreline.

Spiritual teachers do not care if you like them or not, only that you wake up to the love. That is all a true teacher of Light desires, to assist us wake up and become strong swimmers in the Sea of Eternal Love. They are like the gladiators of life guards, strong enough to come back for those who are caught in the rip tides. Connecting to their consciousness lifts us up so that our own consciousness can become one with Spirit and dissolve any negative illusion that would prevent us from swimming deeper!

I have a friend who is so filled with Light and not many around her seem to be aware of who she really is. When I first met her I recognized who she was and my love for her was deep and immediate. It is a different kind of love from romantic love, and yet it can have a profound affect upon us, as does romantic, passionate love when first experienced. When we meet someone and see and feel their Light, our love is immediate and real. Our friendship and love is pure and we do not expect anything from each other in return, just to *get* to hang out with each other is always a gift.

Love, especially romantic love, can be a challenge in Level Two as we truly desire to love others from a place of spiritual love, however we still have fear and expectations for love to be returned in a certain way. We may not as yet have embodied the fact that we have ALL the love we could ever require in a million, trillion life times right here in the Sea. At Level Two we still feel a need for reciprocation (even if we do not think so) when we give a gift or do something for someone. We may still be trading - expecting something in return and this can bring down our power and oscillation when we are first swimming in the Sea. It is so important to learn to love from a place of not expecting so that our consciousness will be raised to higher Levels.

So how do we discern whether the love we are giving whether in romantic relationships, gift giving or doing some action for someone is human loving or spiritual Divine Love?

One of the simplest things we can do is to ask, *Do I expect reciprocation?* If we do it is human love, not Divine Love. (Or finite love, not Infinite Love) We cannot feel deep fulfillment and peace from a gift or from expressions of love given when we know the person is expecting something from us in return and visa versa. The love that gives true satisfaction and joy is the love where we did not expect anything in return. This love comes straight from the heart with no desire or thought of reciprocation. This can be our guide. When we truly give love in any form whether through act or gift and we do it from *not expecting* anything in return, it is pure and beautiful. We have already received, as we have received the gift of *getting* to give and to love. We can take no credit for the love we give because we have come to realize in our hearts, that the love we give comes from Infinite Love, not from our human self who is always being a scallywag and expects *so* much in return. Doing our best to not project into the future when giving serves as a powerful

132

tool. This is living in the now and it is the power of mindfulness.

We can also use *this guide* in our work. If we do our work without needing or expecting anything in return but the pure fulfillment of doing our very best we will be successful. It is in doing a job well that we receive the fulfillment and so it is with love. When we can love another simply to be able to have the gift of loving, our life will always be fulfilled and disappointment will vanish from our experience. The trick is to have no attachment to the outcome and live in the now. Make each *now* special.

I recently received some beautiful flowers from a friend and had no idea I was to receive these flowers and my heart was so truly touched by this beautiful gesture, this gift was a gift of simply giving and filled me with such gratitude and joy. The more we love with no thought of return we will find that all the love and rewards will come to us anyway and more powerfully because we did not love or do our work for reward only. We no longer live a life only to get. At Level Two we oscillate between these feelings quite frequently so before we do anything just ask, *Am I really loving this person or doing this act or giving this gift as a trade? Do I want or expect anything in return?* This is a powerful question and will alter our actions dramatically.

Now let's talk about those rare gems who truly come from Divine Love. There have been Teachers in our time who teach, simply because they love, and live in human form only to assist us to wake up to the Light. To be close to Enlightenment is very rare and precious. We do not always recognize these Divine Teachers nor even get to meet them. We can experience their Divine Love and receive their gifts of higher consciousness through their teachings (esoterically) even if we are quite clogged, we can still be raised up and feel better even when we are not aware of why we feel good. We recognize these

Teachers with how our heart opens up when either in their presence or when we read their words. There is no way to explain it. We just know and feel that this teacher is the right one for us at this time. That is what happened to me. To find an Enlightened Teacher, and then be so blessed that they will agree to teach you is a miracle in itself. For all the studies and reading and searching is nothing compared to the Light (Shakti) Transmission you receive from an Enlightened Consciousness. This is what awakens us so quickly and melts away, like molten gold, all of the old beliefs and attachments etc. The energy is indescribable. We MUST have energy to awaken and have success in our lives.

I have been truly blessed and privileged to have had such Teachers who have led me to the path of enlightenment. Gold light flows from Enlightened Teachers (see Level Five) but if we are too *clogged*, we do not see the Light or know that a Divine Presence was actually beaming right there in front of us. We may have no idea that true Enlightenment is there and yet we can still *feel* their Light! Some feel quite intoxicated, giddy and become over talkative after being in the presence of an Enlightened Being. Put it this way...Remember how it feels when we are first truly in romantic infatuation/love now add that feeling... say a million times and you will get a glimpse of what this feels like. This is Divine intoxication. When the vibration is one with the Divine.

You stand there with tears of bliss while others just walk on by. To feel and actually see everything begin to dissolve in gold is an experience that takes us to the *real* world. The Light from the Sea of Eternity is *amazing Grace*!! May this book and the intention behind it assist us all to *see* and *feel* Divine Love. Let this love shine through and out into the world, and then we can experience heaven on earth as the veil disappears. We all have Enlightenment in us but so few ever become One. But It is real and It is here and It is possible!

I have also been blessed to be acquainted and to work with beautiful teachers, though they were not all at Level Five, but they were still very strong swimmers in the Sea. When I knew them, some were at the time not prosperous, so those who found out or who knew them just a little, would say behind their backs, *How can they be teaching about this stuff if they are not rich?* And then later down the road these teachers sold millions of books and were known throughout the world. These same people who knocked and judged them would at every opportunity say what good friends they were with so and so. These teachers/authors had prosperity consciousness and knew that there is no time, there is only now and they did not let appearances sway them from teaching and living prosperity principles. They knew they were already prosperous and that the illusion of time or appearances would not change Truth. Truth is not about appearances in this *Maya*; it is about consciousness. As Wallace D. Wattles said in "The Science of Being Great", *"When we do small things in a great way, in that certain way, soon we will become great."* And he meant that the greatness in us begins to express itself *through us.* **This greatness is *The Divine Presence.***

This Presence is flowing through as Grace. God's Grace *is* the greatness in us; we are simply the vehicle that this Grace flows through. I know this topic of judging the world and others is sounding redundant but let us visit it again, because if we *really* desire to swim to Level Three, releasing a judgmental attitude is vital. We must not judge by anyone else's appearance. We do not know what they are going to be doing in the next moment or who they really are. It might be in a nanosecond that their lives and success revs up. Like wow, whoosh. But at Level Two, we do tend to judge where people are at in their consciousness by appearances. Why? Because we want to feel like we are progressing and we think it helps if we think we know where others are at. This judging attitude is the ego and the ego is such a self righteous, bratty, and often funny delusion to Truth!

Releasing judgments will also help us to release once and for all the competitive state of mind and become more conscious. As mentioned before in this book, a simple way to see whether we are rising in consciousness is to notice if we are becoming less reactionary and this also goes for noticing if we are less judgmental. When we react our ego is still in power over our lives and is projecting thoughts by reacting. When we notice and allow ourselves to be an observer to what is going on rather than a reactor we will raise our consciousness. It is an excellent way of gauging where we are at. Just BE in the moment before we react and then our actions that follow will be right actions.

When we are judging and being reactionary, we are also into comparing and competition. We may wonder about, *Who is more spiritual? Was my prayer the prayer that worked for that person? Is my faith stronger than so and so?* If we have at any stage of this reading thought to ourselves... *WOW I know someone who is a little negative and who REALLY needs to read this book.* We may be judging that we know what someone else needs. That's OK laugh at this. If, however we wish to mention this book because we feel it may serve another, well that is different. We do not know who is more spiritually aware or less than another; we have no idea sometimes who is *really* standing right in front of us, sometimes in front of our very own mirror just waiting to come forth in all of God's Glory and Grace!

These kinds of conflicts in discernment as mentioned can come up (though not in everyone) at Level Two, but generally this is a fun and very freeing time as we experience more love and go within. We are beginning to release our old ways of thinking and we now have much deeper, intimate friendships with like-minded people who before we would have dismissed immediately from our spheres, based on our surface, shallow judgments i.e. their income, age, appearance or background. We now have realizations and have fun finding the parking spots we want. Money, opportunities and fun experiences start coming our way and life is becoming more joyous and more meaningful. And so Level Two is a good place to be. At this stage of the world's evolution, not many people even experience Level Two.

A word of caution: When we are at Level Two, we must be disciplined in our daily practices if we wish to swim deeper into the Sea of Eternity and become more mindful of what we are thinking. We do not wish to go back to the mesmerizing shore. Inertia may set in at this Level if we allow ourselves to become to cocky. If we go back to the shoreline through laziness and inertia sets in it will be very painful because we don't really live at that shoreline anymore. It is OK when we don't know, but when we *do know* that there is more than our bodies and attempt to live back where we were, then we could live very unhappy lives. We may think it would be easier to go back to that place, before we had this new awareness, but it just isn't. If thoughts of swimming back to the shallow safe waters come up, NEXT those powerless thoughts as it is only our old thinking or ego attempting to distract us and thwart our good. Realize old thoughts do not hold any power. The only power there is, is God. At these times if we go within and contact our Divine Presence all will be well.

Now remember we are keeping it very simple in this conversation, we may be calling these experiences Level One, Two, etc., however there are thousands of mind states we go through to raise our vibration to higher Levels. We are simply keeping it simple in this book, so that we may all have some understanding of what experiences we have been having or may have in the future. Understanding as said, releases ignorance and fear. To explain it in a more simplified way, at Level Two we become aware that we are more than our bodies. And that is a beautiful truth to be experienced. (Beautiful *and* fun, who knew?) We begin spiritual practices, and we experience new heights of awareness; we meet with new fabulous, creative people and life has become magical!

How To Find A Teacher: I feel it may be important for some of the readers who are at early Level Two to mention this at this time. At this Level we can be quite vulnerable, our hearts are opening especially now with the veil of duality becoming thinner and more portals opening to Eternity, so we begin seeking teachers and experimenting with metaphysical studies. If someone is *channeling* an entity, it is my suggestion to be wise in your discernment before studying with them. They may have great ideas that you can relate to but a lot of their ideas could be only based in Level One or in a fear based, twisted type of Level Two at best. Of course some people channel some great information such as Seth and Abraham writings but not all are good so be wary. IF they do not speak of meditation and going within then I would not see them again. Meditation is the most powerful and fastest way to reach higher planes of awareness and unity. Oh how our soul sings when It sees us at last sitting still in the silence.

If we really desire to lift the veil of illusion then we need to be discerning about who we study with. The way I always gauged it was if I felt good when I was with them or listening to them and how I felt about 1 to 2 hours after I have been with them. Did I feel my heart opening and did I feel deeper contemplations coming to my mind. Did I feel more confident about my path etc? If I did not feel good or more contemplative then I just knew these were NOT my teachers. I really feel our soul does something within us when we have found our Teacher...we just recognize them...we know it, it is love...

Another easy way is if they themselves seem happy on their path. This is an easy one. If someone is professing to speak about love and spirit and has a scowl on their face the whole time, well perhaps we would do best to look twice before going back to their teachings. I just could never feel right with fear based teachings no matter what anyone else said. Never feel that you have to rely on someone else or make them your God. An awake Being CAN send you Light/Shakti, as my generous, giving, Enlightened Teacher did for me. So yes, others can assist our journey of awakening with their Light but we all have our own Light. It is simply important to remember this, as there is only Eternal Sea and this is our true Source. We all KNOW what is best for us and we all have different personalities and prefer different approaches. But as I said before IF they never teach about going within then I would be very wary. As they may be good people, but to grow we must go within. However if you can find an Enlightened One, then just being in their presence can awaken your Kundalini* when they give shaktipat. This is a Divine Energy Transmission that some call a blessing. It can be given to you remotely but is always stronger when in their presence, even if it is simply hearing their voice on a webinar or telephone. It can change your life forever!

When we've gone through certain challenges in our life we have certain things to learn from certain teachers or teachings, whether they're health issues, money, relationships or soul searching. They are all good lessons *if* the teaching gets us to a place where we can then move into real Truth, the Truth from our SOUL. Let the dead bury the dead. The mystical way is not the psychic way. The mystical way is God teaching us from within, *directly* to us, through us. We do not require a body that does not *know* it is no longer a body keeping us stuck in the *Maya.* Mystics teach Truth directly from God or from Enlightened Masters not through an entity who calls himself, Fred, Martha or George the Great!

*Kundalini is the Holy Light, the nectar of the Divine that lays dormant at our root chakra. The awakening of Kundalini is the next evolution of humankind. For more info see www.MysticalSuccessClub.com

So, getting back to more experiences in Level Two... After a while at this Level we may come to realize that sustaining the continuous mind practices to have a good life has become hard and a little exhausting. This is when we can begin to actually go backwards and some of us may become despondent and even angry. *Why is it so hard now when at first it was so much fun manifesting and getting the great car, more money, better gigs, opportunities etc.; what is going wrong?*

And then, something happens. All of a sudden, we may feel like strangers to ourselves, we look within and feel unworthy or a fraud to all of our so called *spiritual insights* and *understanding.* This is because we have not yet started deeper spiritual practices and regular meditation, we have only really dabbled a little, just got our feet wet. We have allowed our minds to be the only focus instead of the inner silence. We lose energy if we only use our mind, we must fill up again by allowing the Sea of Eternity to feed us with Light. This Light is *power*; GOD POWER and then we can allow this power to set things in motion into the deeper Sea Levels. We set our intentions and let go, knowing that **God's Grace** is our *fuel* and **Source** of **Power.**

Now let's swim deeper into the Sea of Unlimited Consciousness at Level Three...

Level Three
Our Soul Connection

Our Soul *is* our guardian angel, our observer *and* our inner voice.

We now enter the Sea at Level Three because we have begun to practice meditation and open our hearts to **God Mind** instead of our own human brain and *will power*. Remember we do not meditate, Eternity meditates us. that is why we call it practicing meditation until we have the real experience as I mentioned earlier on. Good to remember. At Level Three we have realized that if we only rely on our human mind to attract success and money and to release sorrow from our life, we will soon exhaust our energies and begin to enter an attitude of, *I give up, what's the use?* So we begin to practice meditation with the intention of connecting with our beautiful soul and hence allow God's Power to lift the veil of illusion. The mind can never help release the mind, so we have to go deeper into the core of our being through the blissful silence.

We now begin to *see* and *feel* that it is not so much that *we are* attracting good but that our good is already here and will appear by letting go, surrendering to the Sea and by going within. As we begin to clear away even more clogging from our heart and emotional body through practicing meditation, we become very sensitive to our inner emotions. Things from our past come up *out of* our emotional bodies. Memories that we had pushed deep down inside our subconscious begin to emerge. When we do this after so many years of having pushed down emotions it can begin to feel very, very uncomfortable. We have attempted to release certain negative memories and emotions, but all we have done is block them, push them down and we have been using sheer will power to move forward in life. Yes we may have been creating what we wanted, but now, through meditation practices and the renewing of our minds through mindfulness and positive intention and affirmations, etc., the cells in our bodies which hold all our memories, begin to open up as the ice (clogging) around our cells and our past hurts and attachments starts melting away.

Here is where we may stop our meditation practices as we do not feel good and we were told if we meditated we *would* feel good. However in the early days of meditation practice as we sit still, these memories we thought we had long forgotten begin to emerge and disturb our inner peace. This can happen more and more frequently at first. Here is where we are looking within and if we continue with our contemplations of God and meditation practices we can begin to go through what has been called *the dark night of the soul*; and *dark nights of the soul* are NOT psychological human depression, they are much deeper and yet they do lead to the Light! Some people say to me, *Well Michele, I began to go into the silence and all there was, was a million thoughts.* This always happened as when we first practice stillness, all the thoughts that were ALWAYS there are at last seen. It is shocking to us; however this too will quiet down.

Human depression can be caused through any number of life experiences or chemical imbalances; however a *dark night of the soul* occurs when we have already done perhaps months, or for some, years of spiritual practices. The waters where we now swim have melted down enough of our old paradigms (negative beliefs) for us to be feeling Light at an intensity that we have never before experienced. This Light is bringing us to deeper Levels of the Sea and this is great. Our ego at this point is holding on for dear life and is afraid it is about to be annihilated and will push us to give up. We hear it say: *Stop this silliness it isn't working, it feels bad to meditate, you have been good for so long you now deserve to take some time off from all this spiritual stuff, you're supposed to let go, right? So let go! Go and have a pizza, watch some TV, have a glass or two or three of wine...* What a naughty child our ego can be when it is afraid of being left behind. It gives us these very - at the time - justifiable reasons to give up. It may not feel that way at the time, this ego voice can sound quite sound, but if we wish to eventually dissolve into the Sea we must refuse to listen. The thoughts we hear can sometimes sound as if it IS the Divine speaking to us, however be very careful as the maya/illusion is tricky and can make it sound like it is our very own story or inner voice. If the thoughts are attached to emotion and it is not a very subtle feeling, then it is still your very clever mind, NOT the Divine. Instead, listen to the *real* inner voice, which is silence. Now this does not mean that we do not have fun and experience some time off but it is *what we do* that makes all the difference. Take a walk in nature or exercise, go visit some positive friends, read a positive book, dance to some uplifting positive music!

If we NEXT our ego's attempt to keep us mesmerized and do not block these past hurtful memories, we will begin to look at what we have done in our past and no longer know who we really are. We may have always *thought* of ourselves as fairly decent, good people, on track with our goals and life plans, and now begin to feel unworthy as we remember what we have done during our life. We begin to feel deep anguish and pain as we start to recapitulate every little event or action from our past that may have caused another pain: *Look at the things I've done in my life that weren't good. What about when I judged, I lied, I did this, and I hurt that person?*

We can feel devastated by our past actions. We feel guilt and shame at the smallest hurt we ever bestowed upon another, even down to when we were a small child and said something nasty to another child. We feel worthless, *Who am I? Who am I to think that I know anything about God or spirituality? Who am I to judge or know anything about Light? How dare I assume that I know ANYTHING about God! I know nothing, I am nothing!* We will cry and within the depths of our being feel too unworthy to be forgiven, *I am so sorry God for I have failed you. I, who am not worthy enough to even ask, ask for you to forgive me.*

Beseeching to God in those moments is often called *the dark night of the soul* and here is where we truly swim into Level Three of the Sea. This, as mentioned, is not human depression; this does not last long for if it did last for long periods it would be depression, so please do not confuse the two.

One of our Mystical Success Club™ Members, on one of our weekly webinars, shared with us all that she had at last discovered happiness. She had been in depression and the Light she receives each day through being a mystical success club member had at last melted away her depression and her gratitude was beautiful. She said that she just sat down for over an hour crying in joy and gratitude. She had never before felt true happiness before. It is only the dark that causes pain and where there is Light the darkness cannot exist.

When we are depressed the thoughts we have, go something like this: *The world did this or that to me, if only I had better parents who believed in me I would be a success now! All this sh... I am experiencing is all their fault, my husband is the one who has been holding me back...* And on and on and down and down we go during depression, blaming everything and everyone else, whereas in a *dark night* experience it is *us* taking responsibility and this is actually quite healthy as we are *waking up* to the fact that *we* have been the cause of our sorrow, not anything or anyone outside of us. HOWEVER if we do not continue to melt away the ice though mindfulness, gratitude and meditation practices we can in fact go down the rabbit hole into depression.

So it is vital to keep going even if we feel we have had a weak meditation, for our beautiful and very patient loving soul knows our intention was good; so if we continue to practice meditation, we will be moving to higher Levels of unity in consciousness even if we do not *feel* it as yet. My beautiful Teacher of Light says there is no such thing as a *bad* meditation and that is so true. I prefer that to *weak* meditation as sometimes it just feels bad, like nothing is happening especially when we first begin to *attempt* to quiet our thoughts. Meditation *does* work if we do the work. Not all meditations at this Level will feel great but it is still working, so never give up!! Here we may still be practicing meditation not really experiencing it fully. The real peace that *passeth all understanding* will come, so keep going...because when Eternity begins meditating us then it is pure bliss!

You may now remember where certain parts of the Old Testament were written during someone's *dark night* of the soul, *I who am not worthy*. These writers were describing a spiritual awakening which the *dark night* experiences are. We are taking off the layers of ego. Going from duality to oneness. So the ego will do its best to hold on as we go within and take the ugly layers of duality off.

Some people will go through the *dark night* more intensely than others but most DO go through it to some degree at Level Three and we must go through a letting go of the human self right through until Enlightenment. As we wake up more and more to Truth we have the pain of releasing our human Level One egoic self. As mentioned this is our ego melting away and it is a great thing for we are opening to God and our small self (ego) knows and does not want to be killed off, which is exactly what is happening - see it is smart, but it has no power other than to play with our thoughts. We have to in these moments learn to be kind to ourselves. This experience is GOOD, very GOOD as now we are connecting to God at our Soul Level, and this is such a powerful experience.

Not all things feel good when we sincerely desire to know and love God. Some things have to be felt to be released; otherwise we are putting icing on an unbaked cake. Yuk!! We need to bake a little more and this is a time when we must draw all the faith we have and continue our meditation practices and mindfulness with a much more dedicated attitude and discipline. Our soul is relying on us to keep swimming, otherwise we may begin to swim back to the shores or get caught in more riptides. We simply allow ourselves to go through it and as we go through these experiences we will find (as long as we continue our spiritual practices daily and remember to have fun!) that we *will* come through and feel such love and exquisite ecstasy. We will feel so much gratitude and our lives will become one of wonder, joy, peace and love. We will go back and forth quite a bit now between Level Two and Three but eventually we will move forward much faster if we persist with our daily meditation practice, gratitude and mindfulness practices.

This is a time to throw out everything in our lives that will attempt to detract us from the Light. If we truly wish to keep moving further into deeper waters of Light then here are some suggestions: Throw out the TV set and only go on the internet when we really have to. Go offline when we are not using the internet as otherwise we will be connecting *energetically* to everyone else online. The same thing with our TV sets, turn them OFF when not watching. TV will keep us mesmerized to the world coma. The internet is a sucker of Light and energy as is TV. If we do keep our TV's please, PLEASE only watch positive TV shows or better still record and watch the shows we want to see later when others around the world are not also tuned in. Also watch DVD's that are powerful, positive thought provoking films - that is if we must keep our TV! Take time to be alone every day and feel the silence within.

Remember these are only suggestions. But if we are really earnest, we will do whatever it takes to move forward and become strong swimmers. We will release from our lives all temptations that could slip us back into inertia. We do not wish to block our feelings by mesmerizing ourselves with hours of useless *stuff* that will clog and distract us from our path. Let's walk in nature and contemplate, meditate and allow our beautiful soul to speak through us in the silence. After a while, we will find what we used to find fun actually boring, dull, passionless occupations. We will still have fun, balance and enjoy life beyond words, but in joy, as opposed to fleeting human happiness. So please do not think this is a time to be *endured,* but rather a time to be gratefully experienced. It is worth it, oh yes, is it ever! Fulfillment, peace, joy and pure bliss are on the way. Then all the good things in life will be added to us. We never feel over excited nor do we feel depressed, we simply feel peace and joy simultaneously. When this begins to be felt more and more often, it is strong indication that the Light is meting away the old paradigms.

Let us now cover a little more of these *dark night* experiences and how we can get through them. When we are having deeper contemplations of our soul connection, this going within will bring up old stuff and we could be feeling that we are bad and unworthy creatures as discussed. Perhaps because we are no longer manifesting like we used to, we may begin to have thoughts that all of these spiritual practices are a waste of time and useless. This again is our ego being a scallywag. These thoughts do not belong with our soul and our ego knows this. Our faith seems to be wavering because things in our life experience may seem to be going from bad to worse. We wonder what has happened as when we first swam into the Sea at Level Two, all was manifesting beautifully, left right and center. We may cry: *Why? Why are things not happening? I love God, I am doing my affirmations, and I am doing my spiritual practices. Why?* But were we? Were we really? If we take off the layers and really look within we may find that we had in fact become lazy.

If we come into Level Three in this way our *dark night of the soul* will be pretty intense as we are still focusing on *what we are not getting* from the world and as the layers come off we will see how fearfully we have been living and it will not feel good. We may have been relying on our thinking alone and felt that our brain/mind was the power doing all this manifesting. We were not realizing it is only the Divine Presence within us that does the work; of ourselves we can do nothing. We had held on... instead of letting go.

What can we do? Now we begin to set strong intentions of what it is we wish to experience and continue to feel as we did in Level Two, that they have already happened, that what we wish to manifest is here right now and then instead of holding these intentions we let them go and meditate into the silence...just let go...ideas and solutions *will* come to us *after* we have felt a peaceful knowing feeling, that all is well. We can then be guided by our higher self as to what actions to take and we take these actions with confidence and mindfulness.

We also learn to be not attached to the outcome as we go about our daily work. We *do not* continue to hold these intentions after we get this *all is well* feeling, but *we do* take action, but action with no attachment to the how, or the outcome. There is only the present, only this moment. We discussed this when doing our daily action list. Our moments *now* will then stretch into the next moment and each action we take will become more powerful as when we do things with all of our attention in the moment we are with our Higher Real Self. We are one with God. God does not live in the past nor in the future. We become one with God Power when we are here NOW! The work we do to keep our mind focused on high in this moment creates a brighter future. But how our future is experienced depends on where we are in consciousness now. Time is the greatest of illusions. Each moment do our best to be really present. Dazzle NOW. From

Webster's dictionary *"Dazzle: To overpower with light!"* How cool is that?

When I went through my first *dark nights of the soul* they were so intense and felt so painful that I did not think I would survive. It was well worth the pain as the bliss and light after is a path to true awakening. Once through the dark side of this experience it transmutes eventually into pure bliss which cannot be described, however if it had to be put into words it is; bliss, joy, love, compassion, humility, wonder and a love for others and all of life so deep that it is beyond comprehension. Sometimes the feeling can oscillate between an ecstatic feeling and sorrow and then go to full out unbridled pure joy and wonder! I have just re-read this explanation and realize that words can simply not describe IT! Oh well I guess you will just have to experience the bliss for yourself!

Because I did not understand what was happening to me when I first began experiencing *dark nights* I thought I was in a depression and began to feel so unworthy as all I desired was the Light Stream...God to purify me with The Light Stream. If you read "Pistis Sophia" (see end of this book for suggested reading) this will become clearer to you as matter, which is human form, is unconscious and it feels so heavy and painful when we begin to feel the Light of Eternity. This is one of the great mysteries.

These dark nights do not usually go on for longer than a bad night or two but they can be very, very intense. When we come out of them it is as if a Light has come on inside and we feel truly one with all life. If I had but known what I know today I would have worked much more diligently on my meditation practices, but I didn't know then, that the best thing I could do was to no matter what, keep up my meditation practices. When I hear people now say that they do not *feel* like meditating and are waiting until they feel better I simply say that *you WILL feel better after you meditate.* Do it NOW especially when you don't feel like it.

I have also heard people say that they will wait to begin meditation practices when they have time to take a month off. Their plan is to go to an ashram in India and do it all in a month. I am sorry but pleeeeeeeease...This is daydreaming to think **one** can cram it all in at once and become **One**! This is not a get rich quick nor is it a fast reading course! But you gave me a good chuckle. It takes months to build up to even being able to practice meditation for one hour twice a day let alone never meditate and then attempt to be in the Silence for a month. You would go crazy with boredom and your thoughts!! I am not saying it can't be done. Nothing is impossible but you would have to be a rare being indeed to never have practiced meditation and then be able to do this. VERY rare. And I have heard this plan from many, many people over the years. Just like you hear *when I win the lottery* etc. It is wishful thinking, as that month never seems to happen. DO IT NOW. Start with 60 seconds six to eight times a day and then build up. After a few months meditation will be part of your life and your life will become extraordinary. You will NOT recognize yourself.

Here's another oldie but a goodie. How do you get to Carnegie Hall? Practice...Practice...Practice...

Back to dark nights...These *dark night* experiences do not last long so do not worry. I kept working on my career, and these *dark nights* would come up occasionally again but then they passed away and the light came on brighter than ever before as did my passion for life and for my work. My work is now pure love for me. I am so very, very grateful that I never gave up. Please remember work and action is not enough. We must also practice meditation. Oh did I already mention that? Has it been a thousand times already?

Meditation is like refueling our car and having the best mechanic in the world tune us up! If we are not refueling often enough from Source, we can go back into wasted fears and worry and empty shorelines. Using sheer will power to keep on going is not enough for any car, eventually we will run out of gas. When this happens we begin to feel literally drained of our life force. As soon as we begin doing this regularly, and eating well and exercising our bodies these dark nights will become less frequent and less intense. I truly did not think I would ever come through them at the time I was experiencing them. Not knowing what we are experiencing is what makes it worse and very confusing, especially when we DO love and our heart and intention is on track. We begin to lose faith. I pray that this book and my sharing with you my own experience will help you to gain some clarity about what is happening so that you will not have to go through as much pain as I did and that you do NOT ever give up!

Once my Kundalini was fully awakened, my process became rapid, as this Holy Light once awakened literally melts away all the old feelings of fear. Bliss begins to feel normal, but until the Light is fully functioning we can still go back and forth. Meditation or being in contact with an awakened one, speeds things along and empowers us greatly. No more drama is needed to be created to feel alive. Life begins to increase IN US, as we become one with life itself!

Gratitude is another powerful tool to use during any experience whether it is depression or a dark night. I read about someone who wrote out a whole sticky note pad filled with Thank You's and then hid them all over her house. I did this but I added a Thank You God in me for so and so... on each sticky note with a different thing I was grateful for. *Thank you God that I can breathe...Thank You God for Success...Thank you God for your love...Thank you God for my beautiful friends Johnny, Lawrence, Bell...* etc. I then put these Thank You

Gods all over my office and home. I put them in the freezer in my clothes pockets, in old books, in amongst files etc. and then when I find one I breathe in deeply and say THANK YOU GOD for... and allow myself about 60 seconds to just be still. I then put this sticky note in my GOD CAN. (A God Can is just that, a canister that you write on that says 'When I can't, GOD CAN!!') This assists in keeping us in the now and not focused on self. I LOVE the sticky note idea and the God Can idea. If I could remember where I first read it I would mention the author of this idea. Whoever you are...*Thank you God for the 'Thank You Sticky Note' idea person... and Thank you God for the 'When I can't, God Can' idea person...*

It is my intention that these words and Light help you understand and release your sorrow and pain. I may not know you in person but we are all connected and I do love you and wish to see you moving into the deeper Seas. It is so very worth it.

The good news is, once I had a spiritual realization of what was happening I was soon back on track. I began feeling so alive and felt so much love it was overwhelmingly beautiful. May these experiences give you more compassion for yourself and clarity. As I mentioned, no one at the time could really explain it to me. I continued to feel lost and confused until It revealed itself. My beautiful Enlightened Teacher did her best to explain all of this however we never really can get it through the mind, IT has to be experienced. The intention here is for you to know that, YES you may still go through these experiences but also to know that there is Light, Healing, Love and so much more, waiting at the end of the dark tunnel.

After we go through these experiences we may return to certain books written by great Teachers of Enlightenment and feel as if we had never before read their words because our soul is now connected - has become one with us and we *feel* the words through our soul, and the love and tears of bliss come rushing forth. Oh what bliss...This conversation was written, in a lot of ways, for us all to understand what the heck these Teachers of thousands of years past were talking about. I thought I understood, but I did not. Truth cannot be intellectualized. I still do not fully understand it intellectually, because it has nothing to do with the intellect, we just feel IT. Oh yes the Love and Light blows me away to bliss and with deep gratitude I thank these Beings of Light who came here, where there is so much sorrow and pain, to pull us out of the riptides. *There are in fact quite a few Enlightened Teachers on the planet today and some of them are actually from the west, so keep you soul open for their call. I guess we all thought they all came from India well maybe they did at first who knows. God knows...*

When we come through all of this, we really feel our connection to our own beautiful soul and know that the Light is within us, *closer than our breath, closer than hands and feet.* We know it has nothing to do with the *human* self - that there's no good or bad, there is only Light. But we still don't feel complete Oneness with God at Level Three but duality is dissolving bit by bit. Yes, we have times, when we do feel such a bright connection and our head buzzes/tingles with Divine Electrical Currents of Light, but only occasionally. We may still be at the very beginnings of Level Three, we may still think of God as someone we pray to. (NOTE: *This deserves repeating often. Please remember there are thousands of mind states we go through. We are keeping it simple here so we do not feel we are all alone within our experiences.*)

Even if we think of God as Light, God could still be a Being that we are praying *to.* When we get past this duality even for only a moment, we can swim into greater Seas of awareness and joy but then we can slip back with the tides. These buzzing/tingling sensations we experience in our brain are the electrical currents from Higher Consciousness that we are now plugged into. As the chakras are opened as the Kundalini (Holy Light) comes up the nerves in our spine and Sushumna-*ethereal spine*, it is like having an electrical power extension that has seven outlets to plug into. As these are plugged in we have access to divine power and other dimensions open up to us. Our brains begin to literally awaken and evolve. The cells of our body literally become cells of Light.

Eternity gifts us downloads of Light and Truth Teachings esoterically. It is like our spirit is now connected at last to our brain. Also our intuition becomes just like a GPS in a car. We know where we are going and are told how to get there. It is The Divine Current connecting directly into our brain and purifying.

I had many experiences where I was shot out of my body into tunnels of Light and entered different atmospheres of what seemed like the stillness of the cosmos and looked like I was in the Universe and a loud roaring and buzzing was heard however I was not as yet completely dissolved at the time in the Light. These experiences although so sublime and beautiful were not permanent. Every time we come back to normal consciousness a little more of our selves is gone. We never come back the same again. We are more of the Light each time until eventually we ARE THE LIGHT. Be very careful if you experience these amazing indescribable events as the ego will at this time attempt to make you feel you have ARRIVED. What has occurred sometimes without us even realizing is we have allowed our ego to take over some control again. And then we might go through another *dark night of the soul* again, *who am I to think that I know God? Woe is me; I'm not worthy...*Why? Because we are not realizing completely that we are an instrument for Light. We do not yet fully realize our God connection at earlier Level Three. But it is much closer... *Closer than breathing, closer than hands and feet.*

After we go through our *dark nights of the soul,* we begin to pray differently, our ego is still there, however it has diminished its power. We let the ego at this Level know that we are not killing it, as it is required to some extent for personality, to help the human body navigate, to drive our cars, to work our computers etc...it is only required as will power until we are truly ONE, it is NOT our higher power, even though it loves to think it is!

So all in all, we can now see it's actually a very good thing to go through a *dark night of the soul.* It is healthy for us to release tears for God. I adore what Sri Ramakrishna said so much I will repeat it: "*We cry about money, houses, husbands, wives, jobs, but who will cry for God?*" That is so beautiful, it is beyond words, it floors me every time I read it! We have been crying in these so called *dark nights* for God and THAT is beautiful. It is good to cry *for* God, not *to* God but *for* GOD. Because what we want with all of our heart is *to experience and know* God. So relax and let go as this is actually a time of Light, but it sure can feel dark! There's no good or bad during this time, what needs to be released is released so that we can FEEL our soul's Light. As long as we don't let ourselves, as mentioned, attempt to block these deep feelings by distracting ourselves - watching TV, drinking, etc., we will come through it and our lives will change forever!!!

During Level Three it is VITAL to keep up our spiritual practices. Crawl to our meditation mats if we have to, meditate, focus on God, on Light. Write out the Thank-You-God-Post-It-Notes! FEEL gratitude in every moment. Use your will power to NEXT thoughts of the past. We spoke about meditation a little in Part One, however here it is stressed that as far as this author is concerned there is no more powerful spiritual practice than meditation to help us connect with our soul. It is in the silence that we swim into the deep Sea of Unlimited Consciousness.

It is also important to understand certain spiritual principles before we begin meditation practices. Unless a meditation has in it a conscious awareness of a spiritual intent, it may not be spiritually beneficial. It can in fact lead to just mental stillness. It is important to know why we are meditating. If it is just to help the physical body be less stressed and healthier fine, but do not expect any true spiritual peace or guidance to follow. We must first bring forth spiritual intent and contemplations on high into the practice to experience higher levels of consciousness. So if we don't feel like getting to that meditation mat, just crawl to it, or sit up straight in a chair, in your car, in the loo, anywhere will do as long as we do it!! Say out loud to help ground us and bring the Spiritual intent: *God's Light illuminates all areas of my experience today and always. I am one with my soul. Bliss and love is here right now in me, as me.* Also focusing on Omnipresence is very helpful. Contemplate what Omnipresence is…and then be still.

A beautiful way to start the day is to be still and breathe deeply and say, *The Divine presence IS with me and I AM grateful and the Divine presence HAS gone before me to prepare the way. I AM God Governed, this day is God Governed.* Another suggestion is to focus on the breath and feel that each breath is actually the heart breathing. Focus on the heart as if IT is breathing each breath. I find this much more powerful than just focusing on breath. The heart chakra can then be stimulated to wake up as the kundalini energy flows up through the chakras.

We of ourselves can do nothing; it is God *in us* that knows how. God is the *only* power. Connecting with our soul helps us to really feel this way beyond thoughts. We are the instrument of God's Grace, but we still may not truly get this so we have to swim deeper. It is so fascinating and beautiful.

When we are going through these experiences we can sometimes feel such love for others that we wish to be of greater service to humanity. This is beautiful because we have melted down a lot of our ego so others become more important to us as we now feel such oneness with all of life. We may realize that the reason we want money now is simply to experience freedom. The *getting of stuff* no longer interests us as much. Money now becomes a tool, NOT a power.

We must take caution here, for at these times if we give everything away we may also be giving away our new found Light and energy and may not be able to be strong enough to swim back to assist others who are still in the rip tides. At Level Three it is good to give and serve others but not to the detriment of our own livelihoods because we are not as yet life guards or even strong enough swimmers, we are life guards in training so to speak. You may say, *I do not want money for myself. I just want money to serve others,* and then we forget we have to pay our rent etc. We could be in a place/state of, I *am not worthy* instead of a place of humility, and be confusing the two places or states. The humility we *think* we feel could play out like this: *I'm not worthy enough but I am worthy at least to pray for another. I don't care if I don't have a good life, as long as I'm serving others.* Can you see that with this attitude we are still praying to an entity we call God? This is not humility. Look within and we may come to understand that true humility is knowing where we are right now; no less and no more than knowing where we are and to also acknowledge that we are instruments of Light for God's Grace. Putting ourselves down is not humility.

So now we have moved through this *dark night* and feel the sunshine again! At Level Three some fears may still show up, yes we *feel* we are connecting to our soul but there is still duality, God and us. This too can hold us back at this Level. We must do our best to not get into why we feel separate and not be tempted to glorify ourselves nor take human pride in our understanding. This may sound like a contradiction but at this Level we go through the whole gamut of thoughts and feelings. All in this Maya, this world, it can all seem quite contradictory. What is seen as good today, tomorrow could be seen as bad. It is all human perception. So just observe these old fears and let them pass away. At this Level peace can be experienced but we are still not one hundred percent present, not the real peace *that passeth all understanding.* And yet we are in a great place so we need to be kind and more patient with ourselves.

There are more highs than lows at Level Three so be happy! The highs are much more frequent than the lows and these highs are indescribably beautiful. But it's not really true peace as it does not last all day 24/7 as yet; but it is a great start, a great place to begin. Many points are being repeated during this book so that we can recognize these not so good experiences at Level Three are not bad and that we are not bad people, so remember to smile. There is no good or bad. It's all perception and it is a choice. We can choose to react or go higher and respond or better still we can simply observe.

We can also at this Level Three, begin to again manifest what we desire, however we are doing it now through intent and letting go, not through our old practices of human brain/mind will power. We are entering a state that has no past or future. The past and the future only exist in our mind and this is where all the pain lives, in the past and future. We are becoming one with the place of Light where there is no time. The veil of illusion is being lifted so the things we wanted are now appearing from the timeless dimensions. They were always there, we just could not see them. So now we see that we were never actually attracting *stuff* to us, *stuff* was always here. Be careful to not judge our spiritual awareness on what we are or are not manifesting at this Level - nor how. We will, with further meditation and contemplation, practices swim to deeper Seas and have great and beautiful illuminations of Truth revealed. We can have a cup of Earl Grey together and giggle about it later.

With the dangerous riptides behind us we can now dive deeply into Level Four...

Level Four
Becoming mermaid/man

Now we dive into the fathomless depths and swim as mermaids. Now we are at home in the Limitless Sea. *Mer* means both Sea and Love. This is why the Sea is often seen as a symbol of Eternal Consciousness.

(As it has been politically incorrect - but never the less done in the past - to put all genders as he or him, please permit this author the indulgence to put it as she, as in mermaid for the rest of this chapter.)

As mermaids we can teach others to swim because not only are we strong enough swimmers we have now adapted to the Sea and swim as if we were born to it, fishtail and all. We can go back to fish out others in the large waves and riptides, as we are now lifeguards-in-training of the Sea. We can simply bask in the exquisite beauty of the Sea with no fear of drowning or getting tired. We can breathe underwater and we are at h**om**e. (OM or AUM) Now that we have gone through the *dark nights of the soul* we feel unconditional love for all creatures and are as comfortable swimming in the Sea as if we were never parted from it. NOW the happiness and Light we feel comes easily. Our meditations are so beautiful that we weep tears of joy. This is truly the meaning of crying for God.

When we first come through we feel as if our whole being is dissolving into everything and we are at one with this love, we are swimming in the Sea of Light. My experience will be different from others as will yours. I know that I started counting the days when this first began as my old thinking was wondering if or when the *dark night* was going to commence again and if I would go back to feeling unworthy, but twenty days passed and then sixty and then one hundred and then two hundred and so on.. until one day I stopped counting and felt home in God. And then, I experienced another kind of *dark night* however this time it was only with a sorrow that I was not as yet ALL of the time in this Pure Light. It was a dark night that was combined pure joy, love, gratitude and yet still sorrow that I was still too often human. But then that too would pass.

I think perhaps until we reach true Enlightenment we will continue to have some sorrowful moments, not really *dark nights* per say, and this could be because we have tasted unity but it is not 24/7. Until the human self has gone it is only natural that the human part will still be somewhat heavy. But the good news is at this Level all we have to do is STOP, breath, open our hearts and *be still* to feel our Oneness. We truly know now we are NEVER alone.

The tingling vibrations we once felt on our head now occurs ALL of the time like a vibrating, soft cloak of radiating light we wear all over! Our Kundalini is now truly awakened and six chakras are open. (one to go) We now feel such deep love, joy and gratitude and pure fascination with how much love there is *everywhere!* We now only have fading memories of what our life was. And it is rare to now ever think in the past. It just does not seem to come up in mind. We now only think of the past for the necessity of using it for some work we are doing or to remember a time of empowerment and bring that Light here and now to support and empower what we are NOW doing. We can remember, but we do not feel as much association or pain connected to the memory. It is a feeling of non-attachment and yet we FEEL more love than we could ever have imagined for all of life and others. We now know we are truly one with everything and that now is all that we have. Time seems invisible to our senses. Living in each moment is where the bliss comes from. This is where the source lives. Every moment is felt as a **continuous moment. We are in the timelessness.**

As mentioned, the experiences can be different for everyone. I can only speak of my own experiences and have confirmed with others I have met on my journey, who also had similar experiences. I was so curious during my experiences to know if others too had these visions or head buzzes. I just wanted to know it was not some medical condition☺. When I was at Level Three, as I mentioned before the head buzzes or tingling are The Divine Current entering our brains. This can happen through an Enlightened Teachers Consciousness assisting us or through enough meditation practices. As we meditate and contemplate Truth and what God is we can feel a heat rising and our bodies become quite hot. (Quite different from hot flashes girls.)

This heat is the kundalini energy rising up through the chakras. The energy has been asleep coiled at the base of the spine or lower base chakra and when it is awakened it rises. I have had nights where the heat was burning to the extent I would have to go and complete my meditation sitting in cool water as my chest would be on fire as would my scalp. At this Level the buzzing is over our entire skull and face and our third eye feels like our entire forehead is open and exposed. It is all beautiful even if it does not sound like it. I told you it is so challenging to explain this in words. Our third eye and crown charka are opening. The more we experience the kundalini heat the more the cells of our body are being transfused with Light and our cells are actually beginning to transform. We are changing from the inside out and from the outside in, but we're not there yet kids.

I have been blessed to have Enlightened Teachers help me, in the human form and without. (And please let's not get confused here with channeling entities who do not know they are dead.) Enlightened teachers can come to us after they have left the body and some never had bodies. Some call these beings Guardian Angels. We can ask in our contemplations for a Teacher of True

Enlightenment to come and help us and they do if we are sincere. We all live in the One Soul the One Sea!

Now is a great time for raising our vibration (which we can only do in the now! How Zen this all is.) and our spiritual practices will now seem like a rare and precious gift that *we get* to experience. Our daily practices actually give us power, peace and wisdom from within as we learn more and more to trust and surrender... to truly let go and let God. This now feels as normal as taking our daily shower or dressing. We now look forward to connecting with and contemplating the qualities of Spirit and become truly *awed* and so very humbled that this awesome love is being transmitted through us. We no longer *have to* use will power to meditate; it is now an honor and privilege that we *get to* meditate. Here we are allowing the Sea of Unlimited Consciousness to *meditate us*. We just connect and allow it to happen. Now we have to use our will power to stop meditating and get to work!

To not meditate and connect with Spirit would be almost like leaving our home without wearing any clothes or brushing our teeth. (I actually like to brush my teeth before I meditate. Whatever works do it.) Connecting to the Sea is now a gift. We wake up in the morning and cannot wait to breathe in God's Light. We realize that our bodies are simply an instrument of Light. We know that we do nothing but allow the Light to flow through us and allow God's Grace to be the Teacher. Anything we say to another is not important. What is important is that the vibration behind the words is from on high and then what we say will be the real communication transmitted *through us.* Vibration always tells the story. We do nothing but allow ourselves to be instruments of God's Grace. We know that this Grace is blessing everyone, everywhere we go and yet we have no ego about it. If we do begin to have an ego about it, we will quickly go backwards because as soon as we bring in the *it is me doing it* we have disconnected. If this happens we simply allow it to dissolve and connect again with the real I that is expressing THROUGH us. We are simply the vehicles.

Think of it this way. If your friend was driving a Volkswagen you would not say *OH here is Volkswagen she has arrived.* No we say *here is Kim*, Kim is driving the Volkswagen. This is the same way with God. We ask God to step into our vehicle called Kim, Phillip or Michele. God is knocking on the door of our vehicle waiting to do the driving. Our Higher Self has actually always been there but we have decided to drive the vehicle on our own. Let's unlock the car door and let the Master Driver take the controls. Then we can sit back and observe all the beautiful country side and experiences on the journey.

Another way to look at it - especially for those who think that non attachment may mean non action, is that we are the FEDEX or UPS guy. We show up to work, make our deliveries but it is none of our business at that stage what happens to the packages after. Our only job was to show up, work and deliver. What expectations or surprises happen after is of no interest to us. When we can approach our work and careers in this way we do not have attachment to the outcome. We simply trust and let go.

After this book is written I will be the FEDEX guy and deliver the book to bookstores through various channels of distribution but after you open this package it is none of my business if you like it or not. Whether it is filled with surprise or you yawn. I have no business about that side of the work; my responsibility is to do the work with love, focus and gratitude. I treat my speaking engagements in the same way and my singing. I show up as a clear vehicle and do all I can to be happy and healthy so that we can all have fun and then the message is delivered and what happens after you all go home is none of my business. People have said they felt moved, uplifted and changed at our seminar events but this was THEIR very own consciousness connecting to what was expressing **through me.** Michele is only the vehicle, the UPS gal! As you are!

Ego does not get as much of a chance to interfere at this Level although it will still try, as we do still utilize personality to function. But to get to this Level our ego does not have the false power it once did to confuse our truth and we can see it coming. We may look and sound the same to others and yet we know we are no longer who we were. God's Grace is now our life and our body is the instrument. Yes, we do still have ego but it does not order us around as it once could. The ego really is simply our mind when it is unconscious making us focus on the past or projecting what it thinks is going on in the outside world. It keeps us only focused on our small self, our small i which loves to live in the past and future.

How do we get to Level Four?

This is different for every single soul. For some of us we have been extremely privileged and blessed to sit in the presence of an Enlightened, Liberated Teacher who can blow away our clogged up consciousness, melt it down like ice, so that our Divine Presence is released. But even if we are this privileged to meet an Enlightened Teacher who is actually willing to teach us, it is still up to us to do the work, as even with this awesome gift from Eternity, we can go backwards if our spiritual practices are not maintained.

For a rare few (like Saint Francis of Assisi who went from Level One straight to Level Five) it can simply be a WOOSH from Level One to Level Four and even to Level Five. This is extremely rare but it can happen. Anything is possible. How? Who really knows but God? But these rare souls may have already experienced many past lives where they had already done the work. So now it is simply a matter of the spark being re-ignited. (Perhaps if they went to an ashram for a month) It could be ignited through a simple reading from an Enlightened Teachers word, the first time we practice meditation, a positive song, a film like 'The Matrix,' or 'It's A Wonderful Life' or 'Beyond The Secret', a small child's smile, a dramatic sorrowful experience like a war zone or the death of a loved one etc. It can also occur because we had in our past lives already been at a high Level of consciousness as mentioned and in this life time we simply required a small push to jolt our Light memory. And these memories of swimming in the Sea are not always detailed past life *seeing* memories, (although some do experience memories of *seeing* their past lives) there is simply a knowing, a *feeling.* We just *know* who we were and who we have become and who we once knew, through intuitive *feeling.*

Some of us (like this author) had to work a little harder, but it is more than worth all the disciplines we may have experienced to get here. It is worth it for our LIFE, for our SOUL. Otherwise we are simply wasting our precious time here not to mention our Soul's precious time which is US! But as I have said before, this is not for everyone and that is fine. It's Ok to not want to do this as it takes work and discipline. We are all where we need to be and when we are ready we will know. We will want to go h**om**e. We cannot take another moment of being *soul sick.* We will do whatever it takes.

Even though Part Two is not an instructional guide or lesson book as Part One was, let it now be said for those who would like some guidelines to swim deeper, that one thing that can help tremendously to open our heart to higher Levels of awareness is to **Love God.** If we do not like the word God, call It Love, Spirit, The Sea of Eternity, Divine Presence or Soul. Repeat, using any name you choose: *As A Wave is One with the Sea I am One with God,* and then talk to God as your best friend *God, I simply wish to love you more, help me to know your mysteries and love you more, God may there be more of You in me than me. I am h**om**e in Thee. You are my h**om**e God.* And then go into the silence…you have now set up a beautiful setting for the Divine Presence to enter. Oh how our Soul loves to hear these words when truly felt. We cry tears of such deep gratitude as our heart is now opening and overflowing with the love we are receiving.

Even if we do not feel this love and longing to know God, if we but continue our spiritual practices eventually *we will* feel the connection. Most of us on the path are way too hard on ourselves. Silence and intention is the key to connecting. In the silence we hear God. In silence we *feel* the love. The love cannot be stopped for love is the only power there is. You have heard that God is love, but at Level Four you will know it is true. God *is* love, therefore *we* are love, pure unconditional beautiful Love. *All that God is I am and all that I am is God. All that God has is mine. I dwell in the secret place of the most high.* And not our small i, our "*I*" which is God in us, our, *I AM!*

This may sound strange as it may seem like duality and that we are still beseeching a God outside of ourselves to show us how to love It more. Well again yes and no. Yes, we may speak to God as a separate Being but we are doing it as if we were speaking to our heart. We know that our heart is part of us and yet it knows how to pump our blood, we just trust our heart knows what it is doing, all we have to do is give it the right fuel, rest and exercise and let *it* do what hearts know how to do best - pump life's blood throughout our bodies. Our heart only lives in the moment. We can learn so much from the heart in many different aspects physical and mystical. 5That is why we are doing all we can to be present, meditate and connect with The Divine Presence so that we can be aware and feel God pumping this intense energy which we call love or Light. God in us is circulating and pumping Light in us and through us and this Light is Grace. God is our heart!

Please do remember, as mentioned here many times, there are many vibratory oscillating frequencies at all

Levels, especially at Level Four. Some people say to me, oh Michele I am at Level Four when they are only just awakening to Level Two. BUT always remember you can awaken FULLY to Level Five in less than a moment. Enlightenment is already here. This is rare to have a full awakening, but YES it does happen. Here we are simply keeping it very, *very* simple so that we can learn to be present. The ice of duality is now really melting as we begin to become aware of our home...the Sea Of Eternity.

Sex and Relationships at Levels Three & Four

Everything we do affects every other area of our life experience, it is all connected so this topic on sex and relationships is vital to becoming wealthy and happy. Napoleon Hill the author of 'Think and Grow Rich' said that choosing the right partner will have EVERYTHING to do with our success or lack of it. The mastermind between romantic partnerships can bring us to heights of such connectedness and joy and to great SUCCESS or its opposite. So please do read this chapter.

At Level's Three and Four when we rise in love romantically with another, if they do not love us back in the traditional *romance novel way*, we do not have a so called *broken heart* as we now feel it is a privilege to have the ability to truly love another in this way. We *do* miss the companionship if we part and especially if it was a healthy relationship but if the relationship has to move on we trust that is for each other's highest good. We now realize that we are in good hands, God's hands, and that both hearts are protected by the Light. We do love very deeply at these Levels because now when we love, it is Divine Love, we are actually loving God in the person - even if they do not realize it, we do.

If the one we are in a relationship with does not have this same awareness of Divine Love, the love they feel from us can sometimes be overwhelming as the Light that is shining through us is profound. WE do not overwhelm, the light does, so do not feel too badly if they leave and cannot handle it and wish to move on. If we take the time to choose wisely when we first begin a romance we can then be more discerning.

What happens is as we experience more Light at these Levels we think we can feel or see someone's heart but, we can sometimes be blinded and forget to see who the human personality is behind that heart that we think we feel. We may at this Level simply not be able to discern our own heart and feelings from another's and what we feel is actually our own feeling of love being reflected back to us. Just because someone looks as if they have a loving nature or a good heart does not mean that he or she is awake to spirit as they may simply be having a human experience of doing good and not for higher reasons. This is not to judge but to discern. Some people who do outwardly good acts may still have a lot of personal issues that may be hidden from us when we are so immersed in only the heart. It is wonderful that they are doing good works however there are some very broken beings out there and if we delve deeper it may be different to what we think we are feeling or seeing.

It is not that we do not wish to serve and support someone who has issues, the reason we must be careful to see the whole person is that we can be hurt in ways that may temporally have us swimming backwards as our lifeforce may be somewhat drained by the experience, especially when sex is involved. We have worked so hard with such faith to gain these Levels of consciousness that we MUST do all we can to protect ourselves and not become unconscious.

At these Levels the Light that is shining through us is to serve many more than just one person and so our choice of partner can help our Light shine if we allow our higher self to guide us. My suggestion is to simply wait a while and get to know someone before you make love. Make sure you read more than their looks or personality. All romantic love has its risks however just be a little more discerning before you take the plunge into the bedroom. Remember this; when we make love with someone we are giving that person permission to commune with our whole being and whatever someone is feeling before they make love they will bring into OUR energy. So if you do take the plunge early on in the relationship, please at the very least, PLEASE be aware and sure that both of you are in a joyful, happy vibration.

Remember whatever vibrations are taken into the bedroom will increase and affect both. This is especially true for women as women are in a vibration of surrender and will take on more. This is GREAT news girls...if you have a conscious partner.

Light that is now be transmitted through us does tend to push on the dark shadows of our loved one and can at times feel uncomfortable as it brings up the shadows. They may not understand this so do NOT attempt to explain. They may attempt to explain it to themselves (or the ego will, it's a trickster) and think *you think* you are better than them when this is not even the last thing on your list. You do not have a list, you simply love. You may have not said a word of your spiritual experiences and may wonder why when they seemed so in love that they choose to leave you. (Especially confusing if we are at Level Three) If this happens do not be too sad as God WILL bring right companionship when the time is right. Know that you were there for them as they were for you and silently let God through you bless them and let them go. Be grateful ALWAYS for the gift to be able to love at this depth. It is beautiful.

To love another and have true intimacy is a gift but it does give us something in return...it gives us joy. The past hurt feelings and disappointments we once experienced in romantic love were caused through our need to be loved back in a certain way and for our partner to behave toward us in ways that we have been programmed to look for, *Me man, you woman, so act like this and cook my dinner... You man, me woman you provide for me, pay for my dinner, open car door, treat me like princess...* How funny we are in relationships. But that is not our fault, this is how we have been programmed to think love looks like. We think that to experience love it must be through another person loving us back and that the love must come to us in the way we expect it, the so called *right way,* otherwise *Yourrr...outta here mister!!* Now, we know that this is not real love only human love with no soul uniting depth.

At Level Four (and some at a high Level Three) when a relationship has had its time, we may still love the person however we will be grateful that we had an opportunity to love. We no longer feel the anger but even if we do feel some pain and miss their companionship, underneath any pain there is still joy, peace and gratitude. When we love another the love we feel back from the person is actually our own love coming back to us. This is to love from on high. We trust all things to our God Self and know that if required for our growth a Higher Love is on the way. We can still remember that we once may have felt deep loss when love was not reciprocated in the ways we expected and how we felt crushed, so we have to be careful to not let our old memories dictate to us how we *now* feel. The ego told us we were *less than* if not loved in a particular way. As mentioned the ego can be a real naughty spoilt child! ☺ Going into a relationship with no expectations is one of the vital keys to happiness. If a relationship has to move on please allow it to with love and gratitude.

At last at Level Four we can now love without wanting anything in return only to enjoy the gift of companionship and the gift to *get* to love God through another person and visa versa. It is a real gift when our heart has been so opened by the Light that we can love so freely. We love at our Soul's depth and this is beautiful. Tennyson wrote, *"It is better to have loved and lost then never to have loved at all."* This is true, all except the part *"and lost"*, as we have *gained* through loving, we do not lose anything.

AH, now let's discuss the magical union when we are blessed to meet another soul who truly loves God/Eternity! It is a true meeting of the soul and so very special, rare and beautiful. To be in each others presence is magnetic, humbling and blissful. So love making now can be a meditation in Love and Light. And this is the same when it is not a lover but a beautiful friend who is a lover of Light. Rumi the mystical poet and his beloved friend Shams went through deep pain when they were separated through scheming jealous students. They missed each other's Light, because at last they had met another being who was totally absorbed in love for God. They had no one else who felt the way they did. This path can sometimes be lonely however the rewards and fulfillment are well worth it. Our true beloved is God... that is the true mystical marriage. Oh but when we meet another soul who also feels this... what Bliss and Light can be experienced.

Some may be asking, *What Michele? Would you remind repeating what you said before you started in on Rumi and Shams! Did you just mention sex and romance? Do we date or even feel like this type of romantic coupling at Level Four? Huh... I don't get it?* This is because we have been programmed to believe that spiritually inclined individuals (Lovers of Light of God) no longer feel human sexual passion. Remember the strongest urge God gave us was the urge to procreate. No one would ever wish to create anything if we did not have this urge. We would have no electricity, no art, no music... It is this sexual energy that creates the passion to evolve and to well...create. This urge helps us to feel passionate about life. We do not have sex all the time just because we feel the urge, we are not animals (Although some may disagree), we can transmute this sexual energy into creative endeavors, however it is still sexual energy. Passion gives us the ability to love life and to love God. When we are less clogged by the world's coma type thinking and we begin to contemplate higher thoughts, we are *much more* passionate and receptive creative people.

However having said that we do not *all* feel the need to have sex again at this Level Four as for some the feeling of unity with God is more than enough and we do not have feelings of lust, so to speak, for others as we once did. It is different for every individual. I feel it is far better to not have sex at all unless it truly is an experience from on High and then it will of course be far more than sex. It will be a meditation in Love! You will be guided from on high. Never say never!

I will repeat...We do need to be more discerning with our choice in partners, however there are no accidents in life, so at Level Four whomever we choose to love in this romantic way is for a High Divine reason for both of us, so we trust the connection and let the love flow. We may be in a romantic relationship with a Level Four who could change our life and we are simply too clogged and so used to drama that we do not see nor realize who we are with. We may feel love and passion for them however sometimes be a little uncomfortable and perhaps feel that they are judging us. Our old paradigm will bring up old thoughts as to why we feel uncomfortable and then we could release this person from our lives without knowing that the discomfort we felt was our ego being pushed. Our old beliefs may exclaim: *What no drama, no jealousy they must not love us enough*! When in fact this person was filled with only love, no judging was going on, just loving. Light does seem to push on our ego self. Perhaps we were simply not experienced in feeling unconditional love. If through our ego, which does not like change, we do release this new loving person from our life, they will not in any way cause a drama or attempt to manipulate. This could then cause confusion in us or our ego will confirm that they did not love us enough to fight for our relationship through drama.

Level Four's do not work that way. They trust all relationships and experiences are for a higher purpose and leave it up to God. They love because they were guided to this person, and perhaps recognize the Light that this person is shining and they simply are not as yet aware of it, but it is there, so then they can love God through this person. *Thy will be done*, is their motto as they know that if the person comes back to them it would be through *their* own inner guidance, not through any game playing or manipulation. Now there will be a union made in heaven.

Why, You may ask, would a Level Four be in love with a lower Level? As we grow in unity in love with out God self we love all beings and see that everyone is of equal worth, whatever their Level of spiritual, mental, emotional or physical development. It is the true being, behind the drama that we rise in love with. Light may be required for this person and our higher self guided us to love this soul to assist them to swim into deeper Levels of heart. To wake up to Truth. *We* do not help them wake up, their own consciousness does it. All we have to do is show up, love and let the Light shine through. This attraction can occur without any conscious intellectual thought as to *why* we feel love and passion for this individual, we simply DO. Perhaps it is even an old love from one of our past lives as at Level Four we are more sensitive to that which cannot be seen, only felt. All we know is that we love. That is more than enough and to love is *always* a gift.

We may have been dating a highly aware soul and not even have known it. One of those, *Oh they were too good to be true, never got angry, must have been something seething inside to be so happy, thoughtful and nice all the time,* types. Most of us at Level One - and even some at early Level Two - only feel passion for another romantically when there is some drama or emotional games being played. We are not comfortable with true intimacy. True intimacy does not mean sitting down and breaking down every single little experience together.

Therapy, these days has labeled this as *sharing* or *processing* when most of the time it is simply *throwing up on each other and living in the past.* Reliving the past or projecting into the future instead of living in the moment is sometimes called 'sharing' when often it is just a whole lot of blah, blah, blah, going on...People sometimes feel such ego and confuse it with sharing when all they want is for you to say that they are right and that your behavior is wrong. People say they want closure. No they don't, they want the other person to listen to them, to feel that they are right and you are wrong. That is our ego. Confronting someone to have closure how silly. True forgiveness from within... that is the real closure.

Criticizing someone's past behavior will lesson love NOT strengthen it. They think that unless they get their turn to share that they will not be able to move forward. Move forward to where? Now is the only place to move into. Love is not in the past it is here. Too much processing can actually have us stuck in the past and that is not true sharing or intimacy. If processing all over each other is required to feel passion well watch out, as true intimacy will not be created. Not the true intimacy that leads to real connecting, communication and *spiritual passion.* We do not require a whole lot of drama and emotional highs and lows to have beautiful relationships. We must let go and simply enjoy each other *and* only make love when both partners are feeling connected and happy. (Oh did I already say that. I told you I would repeat these ideas a LOT! Well I guess I am living up to my word...)

I know I am repeating messages here a lot, however it is my job to deliver this message and make sure you sign for the package. If you are not at home I can't deliver your package and can only leave another message to let you know that I was there. I will deliver the package again and hope this time you will be home to receive it! So let's deliver this one again...

We can take on a lot of energy from a partner during sex and so it is vital, especially for women, to be in a loving, unselfish, playful vibration. Some become so in the habit of using drama *to feel* that if there is not some drama being created they do not feel passion or are not *turned on*...The only thing we need to be *turned on* to is Spirit, then all our passion will be directed to a higher love. The love we make, when we make love with another soul, will become an experience that is truly creating more Light and will lead us into higher Levels of consciousness. If we feel passion and real attraction for another and truly enjoy *and* feel good when we are with this person, then if we are patient our heart can open to true love.

Now let's have some fun and have a conversation about consciousness through sex...Sometimes this method is called 'Tantric Sex', however this is only because people LOVE to label experiences that do not have words. So let's forget labels and talk about creating more Light during sex. When both partners practice daily meditation and mindfulness they have more energy and are more in touch with being in the moment. When we have *the intention* of creating more Light then love making can become a meditation in itself. It can be pure bliss.

So how do we experience this type of Light making during sex?
Our focus is to consciously separate the mind from the body while having sex and to let go and join joyfully in other dimensions of Light. For Light to enter our consciousness we must be present in the here and now. We can access these timeless higher dimensions by being focused with love in the present moment. Love making is a perfect time to live in the now and take all expectations out of the mind. In fact take all thoughts out of the mind.

Here are some suggestions to create more Light during love making...Face each other and hold hands. Focus the energy that is flowing back and forth by letting go of thoughts and begin to meditate, after say five minutes of silent meditation, while still holding hands, open your eyes and look deeply into each others eyes while focusing silently on the words *Love* and *Light* or *I*

Love You for a minimum of three minutes (longer if it feels right). Then go ahead and make love and *feel,* do not think, just let your union flow. This will help unify and will help to let go of sexual expectations. This way the positive energy will lift both partners into higher dimensions and create more Light. You will be in the moment and be able to lose all thought. Love making can in this way become a powerful meditation practice.

People must meditate and have energy to begin with and be able to concentrate strongly or it will only be ordinary sex. Our soul takes over using this intention and even if one partner does not have as much energy (and we are not speaking of physical energy although this does help) as their partner, the partner with less energy will still feel good if their intention was right and will perhaps, days later, realize they feel happier and more peaceful than they have in a long time. A lot of giggling could occur and smiling after love making is over, (and during for some.) as the Light is still being transmitted to each other, sometimes for days later.

Intention is the key. To have the intention to create more Light during sex we create more of whatever the energy/consciousness is there to begin with. So if we put ourselves into a high state and meditate before love making we will create more Light and Empowerment. The same is true if our attitude is to just take, with this selfish attitude more selfish vibrations will be created and the partner who was not taking may feel like they were not even in the bedroom. In these modern times we have perhaps read too many magazine articles about sex where the focus is all about having a good orgasm. This leads to performance anxiety and is definitely not conducive to a real loving union of two souls plus it's no fun, it's not being there in the moment. Forget about orgasm and be in the moment with your lover.

This selfish type of *when do I get to have an orgasm* love making will drain the other partner and will later also make the person who did the taking feel slightly depressed without perhaps knowing why. This is just physical masturbation. Why involve another person if all you want is to get off..? BUT when it is with a *high intention* and is playful and loving it will be so much better than just pure animal release. This type of love making is intended to create more Light, and will help tremendously to raise Conscious Awareness.

Gandhi said it all so perfectly, *"Spiritual relationship is far more precious than physical. Physical relationship divorced from spiritual is body without soul."* You may ask, *Why bring up sex and relationships here Michele? I was not reading this to learn about sex...* I just wanted to make sure I still had your attention! PLUS everything we do is connected and affects everything else in our lives, including money and success! Love making has a lot of power and magic when it is with the right person.

How do we know who is at Level Four?

We don't know for sure as there are so many degrees of oscillation and thousands of mind states we go through at all Levels. Each Level of consciousness contains so much and there is a going backwards and forward as well. You know one step back two steps forward and even more in what we are referring to here as Level Four. This is a simple guide, as some of the Eastern books although beautiful, can get very confusing. Also people tend to sometimes take too many things literally and that can get tricky. We have to let the teaching download into our consciousness. I was guided here to speak to you in the way I like things explained...simply. And anyway we can never really explain any of this in words but I sure am having fun and joy attempting it. (with a lot of help from on high)

Some highly aware beings are rock musicians, homemakers, Wall Street go getters, the local priest, or even the gardener at school. So as mentioned over and over again we cannot judge by how a person looks, how much money they have or do not have, nor by their educational background; only vibration tells the story, not us!!

There may be Level Three and some rare Level Four people we have actually met who seem to live, on the outside, quite ordinary lives. Not everyone teaches but these souls are our worlds balance. They are NOT living ordinary lives, their Light is simply inconspicuous to the outside world or to those still at the shore. Some simply choose to live and spread the Light in other ways because through their consciousness their actions are then filled with Divine Light. These people assist governments and the media in ways that they are probably not even aware of. And some do not even know anything about spirituality except for the love in their hearts for God and Humanity. We HAVE to have these souls to have balance in the world. Where they are not present there is often litigation and competition and fear based businesses. If ALL businesses were run only through competitive practices this world would be doomed. These people teach the world by *showing* the world through simply *living it.* We need to have people of higher consciousness in ALL professions to assist our planet. They let their life be the demonstration of love and help without many or maybe any knowing who they really are, maybe not even themselves. Simply by being near them we connect to their consciousness which lifts us up without us even being aware that it is happening. (By the way if you think you are a Level Four stop judging even yourself as this Level may take many, many years of meditation and dark nights to realize. I have met maybe twenty in my whole lifetime thus far… well in this body… but remember we ALL have the capacity to become ONE, every single one of us can do it)

Occasionally but only rarely do we meet such people and all we know is that we love to be with them; they always seem to be happy and playful. Because of what we have been programmed to believe about God loving folks, we often are not aware when we are with these individuals. There may even be a seemingly down and out sort of fellow who is simply going through a *dark night of the soul* and he just needs to re-remember who he is, then whoosh. We do not know, we cannot judge. When we are with these individuals life seems brighter somehow. After we are with them things start working out better in our lives. We may never know that it was the Grace of God flowing through this individual that blessed us that day. And THIS is all a Level Four desires, not to be acknowledged, but for us to feel the Light. They know they can only be an instrument of Light. That is ALL. And yet that is so much. That is more than enough fulfillment. Even though at Level Four we do still have ego, it is just that the ego has much less power and no longer makes all our decisions for us.

We may meet a teacher who's able to transmit Light to us; the Truth of who we are. That Light can come in the form of words, transmitting Light through a teacher's book; a prayer we read and contemplate, or an actual person we meet or simply someone we sit next to on a bus. We may even sit down where they had just been sitting and that is enough Light for us to feel better. Different experiences will occur, when we are ready to swim deeper and have started on a path of self discovery -Yes it sounds cliché, but the teacher will appear, in one way or another, when we are ready. Magic happens when we open our hearts. It may occur because we have sat long enough to meditate and then feel the Light, the Peace.

If we are new to Level Four here are some suggestions to help us to keep swimming deeper: This is the time for those of us who are truly desire with all of our being to lift that veil of illusion when we must do our most vigilant work. We must be so focused and release the things that are going to hold us to this earth plane, to this earth consciousness which is the *Maya*. YES I know you've heard this before in this reading but it is so helpful. Throw out the TV. Don't watch any sort of TV at this time. Do not read any newspapers. Do not go online, unless you absolutely have to, for say, your work. Let's get off the web every time we finish using e-mail or have completed the research we may need for our work. We do not need to have any of those weird frequencies that come from the World Wide Web, entering our sensitive and very open unclogged consciousness at this Level.

We have worked hard to reach these deeper waters so please let's not pull the plug and throw it all down the drain. Be in the silence and listen. Meditate, read illuminating books, listen to positive music. Be in nature as much as possible, take long walks, go hiking, keep hydrated, exercise, be near the water, shower a lot, wash our hands and face with cold water throughout the day. Throw out all the things in our home that are old and that could take us back to the consciousness of our old selves; old photographs of past loves, anything that is going to disempower us and keep us stuck on the earth plane of consciousness. Anything that is going to side track us into the human drama and reminds us of who we used to be.

As mentioned not everyone knows they are at Level four. For some it is simply a deep love of life, love of God and a feeling of joy and wonder. For these individuals they most likely went from Level One to Four, whoosh...from past life empowerments in this world or in other dimensions. For others through simple spiritual practices, they come to know somehow that they are instruments of Light and dwell in God's Grace. All we need to know for now is that if we are really willing to learn to love God and do the work we can swim to Level Four. We may still oscillate back into Level Three, but we won't go back to Level Two or One even if we sometimes want to. Ignorance is bliss?? I think not!

It is important in the early days of Level Four to be aware and notice when the world is causing us pain. We feel with so much heart and compassion that this can drain our energies, however we now know enough to take our physical presence away from all the noise and just be alone with God to regain our strength and become once again grounded in God's Grace/Light. We may need at lot more space, time in nature and sleep than we did even at Level Three especially after being with a lot of people. We may not have yet learned techniques to take lines of energy, others hooks into us, out... We are mermaids now so we simply swim into the deeper Seas to get away from the splashy swimmers for a while. Here in the depths of the Sea there is no noise. Anyone who has ever dived will know to some extent how peaceful it is to swim in the depths of the Sea. So quiet, so peaceful, no rushing about. The fish, we see, are simply *being* fish and happily swimming around.

But at Level Four we are still not fully *one* with the Sea so we absolutely require quiet time and grounding to handle the world's harshness. When we are again rested we can rejoin the world and again allow God's Grace to move through us to bring more Light to those we encounter swimming - sometimes in circles. Once refueled and rested the energy is so high we may need no sleep, sometimes for days. We do not at this Level have omniscience, but we are very intuitive and can tap into God Mind; we are also very psychic at this Level but psychic abilities are an experience of the world, psychic abilities (others thoughts, past, present and future thoughts of others but all still in the *Maya* etc.) are strong at this Level but they are NOT intuitive powers. With intuition (Gods thoughts, out or above the *Maya*) we tap into God's omniscience but it will still come *through us*, not *as us*, at this Level. God does the work, not us. We can no longer take credit; all we have done is allowed our instrument to become unclogged so that it can be an instrument, a vehicle for God's Grace.

It is always important to keep our bodies strong and healthy but even more so at this Level as with strong healthy bodies we can stay grounded and strong enough to handle the Light so that we can allow God's Grace to transmit the Light. We keep our feet on the ground and our head in the clouds, or in the water. (Mermaid's tails disappear when out of the waters; they do this so as not to be recognized. This way they can help others without attracting too much attention. What playful happy creatures mermaids are!)

At Level Four we may have times when all of a sudden we realize and feel that there are only luminous souls on the planet, that there are actually no people. Only beautiful luminous souls that we are connected to. We see that what a person *does,* is not *who* they are. Literally everything may seem just like the film "The Matrix" (awesome mystical film): a world filled with dream walkers; we will see that nothing is real. We see that we no longer have anything to fear from people, places or things...Because God is not in total unity with us at this level of the Sea, we have to transcend mind and thought in order to unify with our soul, our God self. However, unlike "The Matrix" film where they unplug and then enter a life of drudgery and shades of grey in a terrifying *real world* fighting machines, when *we* unplug to the world's coma we enter this beautiful calm, exquisite, bottomless Unlimited Sea of Light and Bliss.

We now also can have fun with our bodies; we can see our body as an instrument. We can have fun and dress it up. Not to impress anyone simply to enjoy it. Sometimes at Level Four we have to play act that our personality is still the same to those who would feel too uncomfortable, especially with close family members who have known us all of our lives. So we do not reveal too much and simply dress up the vehicles called our bodies and personalities in an appropriate way. This actually helps us to stay more anonymous so that we can do better work to help others. We know that we are not better than anyone else as we have now come down off our soap boxes. We know all we have done is unclog enough to let God's Light shine forth. We will do anything that is required of us to shine the Light. Keeping ourselves well dressed and looking good actually helps our Light shine brighter.

It is all about vibration. Better clothes have a higher vibration, a higher energy will be transmitted when we are dressed well, and even if we are at Level One we all know this is true. *All people* care about how they look and when we look good we DO feel more confident. We can have FUN dressing up. We no longer feel an ego-sense of self when we know we look good, it is just as if we were dressing up a doll or buying new furnishings or even a new car. We know we are not our car and yet we look after it as it helps us to get around safely. We are not our bodies any longer - we are a vehicle for Light.

A word of caution: We can have some pretty 'out there' spiritual experiences at this time and be extremely psychic, but let us not get too caught up in these experiences as they will end up fascinating us more than the Light and that could take us off of our purpose and back to Level Three. And DO NOT attempt to speak about your spiritual experiences with others because they may think you are either, one egotistical, two crazy, or three full of sh.. (Unless you have a Teacher who can guide you, just keep it to yourself. Just be quiet and experience the Light and allow it to shine through you...)

Every day let us be happily and gratefully dedicated each morning, after awakening, to our beautiful and extremely patient, loving soul. We know that the Divine Presence goes before us every day and night to prepare our way and make the crooked places straight. We now know of ourselves we do nothing, all we are to do is to stay as positive and bright as we can and always to respect with gratitude this gift of having a loving heart. Now we are going deeper into the Seas at Level Four and we begin to no longer get as drained by the world as we once did. We know there is no good and evil. We REALLY KNOW IT!! There is only Eternity. We are not as yet one with Eternity, but we feel the Light so brightly sometimes our eyes burn with it, it is so bright. Not like sunlight bright, just REALLY BRIGHT and we feel such exquisite bliss.

Look again at the cover of this book, look at the Sea and the gentle waves; this is the Sea we now speak of. It tickles us and we feel our heads softly buzzing/vibrating. It is not a sound it's more of a real physical feeling and each day we notice it is vibrating for longer and longer periods until it is buzzing all day. Sometimes the buzzing is stronger than other times, and sometimes it is as if the hairs at the top of our head (crown chakra) is on fire. This can happen especially when we are doing the work that is helping our purpose or simply doing our work whatever it is, well. It happens VERY strongly when we are in the company of those we are very close to and have begun *rising* in love with.

Now let's discuss other experiences. I do not wish to put labels on experiences however this may help explain some of the eastern terminologies. When I lived in Malaysia I loved to learn about what was possible and I met some wonderful monks who helped me to become excited about what was actually possible for at that time I thought these experiences of Light were only for special chosen ones. We are ALL the chosen ones or we would not even be here.

You may have heard of the eastern term called *Samadhi*, we can, at this Level, go into states of *Samadhi* during our meditations. There are lower and higher states of *Samadhi,* the highest is *Nirvikalpa-Samadhi,* however that is only experienced at Level Five and beyond...in early stages of *Samadhi,* there is a spiritual connection that lies beyond waking, dreaming, and deep sleep. When we are in this state there is a pausing of specific mental activities while increasing activity in other areas of the brain which allows for more conscious awareness to be downloaded to our awareness. That is why we have the beautiful Light buzzing sensation inside our skull. This is the object of meditation: to be able to absorb more Light. However true *Samadhi* goes beyond any bliss we have EVER humanly experienced and way beyond a few head tingles. It is a unified experience in which our consciousness becomes one with the Sea itself. This occurs when all of our other mental activities pause, all except consciousness.

Concentration is not *Samadhi*. Concentration helps us to create a mind capable of experiencing *Samadhi* by *strengthening* our mind. Sometimes we may have Light experiences happen after an actual meditation as the Light is still being transmitted and being assimilated long after the meditation. As it is absorbing, this higher state can occur when we least expect it; hours, or for days after we have meditated. We may be in public and we will feel such bliss and find it hard to speak, stand or even walk; we are overcome with love, and feel such love for every person we see. We can feel as if we actually know each person and at these times, we do. This has happened to me even when at the post office or while sitting in a movie theater. I have had to pinch myself to stay focused otherwise I would be an embarrassment. I am not embarrassed, but the strangers I would have gone up to and told them how much I loved them and how beautiful they were sure would be. After a while we learn how to be grounded and to simply allow this energy to flow out from us and do the good only IT knows how to. The power of this love is beyond our mortal understanding. We can focus this power (Which is Love) into our business, our careers and our relationships.

At other times we will be totally aware that we are not in our body and we find we are observing our body as if it were a doll or a car, totally separate to us. Other times we will be shaken with such tremendous Light and love that our whole being will vibrate and through tears of bliss we will laugh and giggle. Others around us will also begin to giggle even though they will not know why. When we are in these states everything just seems so silly and funny, when we observe everyone taking life so seriously it can be quite hysterical. In days of old we were probably put in the loony bin.

One day a small child of about one, smiled at me at the post office and her heart opened to mine and it was all I could do to not start kissing everyone in sight, her smile was so pure. I said silently to her, *Hello God. please remember, little one, who you are when you grow up*...At these times it is so important to have a strong body that is well nourished so that we can ground ourselves enough to live in this world. I have friends who remind me to eat as an undernourished body will float away and we *do* have to live in this world as well. I am becoming much stronger now, but during these downloads or what some call initiation periods it can be a challenge.

Other times our experience is that we feel everyone's sorrow and feel such compassion that it is almost too much to bear, again at these times we have to ground ourselves. Yes I am repeating myself but through repetition you will remember these words when these experiences come over you. Remember Level Three where we went into high states of love and then into feelings of being unworthy and not being good enough? Well at Level Four we too come in and out of experiences/feelings however it is very different. We now have to deal with two worlds: one of Light and beauty and one in the so called *real world* and then we have to do our best to go about our daily business while still feeling this strong pull to let go and just swim in the Sea.

To live in the world is hard sometimes, but if we are to do any good for others we must do whatever it takes to ground ourselves so we can get things done. We must focus all our first attention (left brain) into doing our daily work and do every tiny detail with total focus and as impeccably as we can, this also helps us to be mindful and to get things accomplished. Now, the projects we work on will be fantastically successful as long as we stay focused and ground ourselves. If we just float around we will never achieve anything that will help us to be prosperous because as mentioned many times **money does serve us in many wonderful ways.** If anyone tells you that money does not help, then they may have not as yet experienced what wealth can do. They say this as it feels better to talk about money in a negative way so that they do not feel *less than* or a failure. We must, if we are still not as yet experiencing the prosperity we desire, keep our *attention* and *intention* clear, do good work, complete projects and let the Divine Presence do the rest.

Sometimes at this Level we may seem overly enthusiastic to people on the outside but this is simply

God tickling us. Others, who can *feel,* will *see it* through our eyes as our eyes are very bright and shiny and sometimes quite rosy in colour. This rosy colour is caused through the kundalini energy and the tears of bliss we experience so often in meditation. Our soul's vibration is felt immediately by less clogged beings. We often have God bumps (goose bumps when not cold) all over when we are experiencing this bliss. Others also will feel these God bumps even if they are at Level One or Two and they may simply think it was something else that caused it, a draught in the building perhaps. This does not matter to us if they do not know the reasons, we are simply happy to see God work *through us* and serve to affect positive outcomes and higher vibrations in others. We know others feel a little better, uplifted when with us and yet we know it is not us, we are the car, the vehicle, the instrument.

Yes, yes I know you have heard this a zillion times by now but it is vital that we never allow ourselves to think it is *us*. The ego can still attempt at this Level to make us think WE are important and special. It is not us, not the *us* we know as Michele, Bob, Paul or John, it is the *I* in us, which is God's Grace/Light. This Light is literally expressing through our instrument out to the world and we feel such gratitude that we can be present for those who want to experience the Light. Even if they are not aware of it they would not have met us if they did not at some level desire better lives, they would have been somewhere else that day.

It is a privilege to be an instrument, a true gift. *But it is never us.* If we EVER feel it is us and that *we* hold the power then we are still at Level Two or perhaps early Level Three, as at these Levels, YES we are transmitting a lot more Light but our ego is puffing us up so that *it* will feel important. What a scallywag that ego can be. Ruffle its hair, call it a knuckle head and shrink it, on its way...

This is also a challenging time when in business with others or with our partners if the appearance of success has not yet manifested, our faith and trust is so strong, we know that God-in-us, is the supplier *and* the supply and we know that all we have to do is trust and keep working on our projects and that all will be well and prosperous as long as we never give up. You may ask, *"What is so hard about that?"* Well when we have others we work with who are worrying about money, the economy, etc., nothing we can say will alleviate their worrying, they do not wish to hear from us, *Oh have faith. Just trust a little longer you will see that things will shift. Our source/God is supplying us with all we require even if we cannot see it yet. All will be well in fact all is well...* No, no, no, they do not wish to hear this, they only want results NOW! All we can do at these times is let them know we are there and will not let them down, we must continue to work hard with love and excellence with our projects, and our business, which is God's business, will demonstrate success.

It can become very draining indeed at earlier Levels when we have others around us worrying, they do not realize that they are actually slowing things down by their fretting plus they are unconsciously draining our life force, even for early Level Fours and especially when we love these people deeply. They do not do this to be mean, they are simply in a worried state of mind. We MUST do all we can to remember in these times that the ONLY POWER IS GOD and that no one's *worried vibes* can stop us from experiencing success. DO NOT speak to them about your faith as this will not serve them it will probably just annoy them. Allow God's Grace to flow through you and into your business. Let THAT be the demonstration of faith.

Turn away from these appearances and keep working and taking action because it WILL turn around. For some of us our work and career goals will shift or change dramatically with this faith. We will know that God is in us, guiding us *always* to right livelihood. Anyone who has ever supported us will also be *very, very well looked after* by the Light. Oh yes indeed they will. Even if they do not believe us, we believe, we know, and we have more than enough faith to carry everyone through *as it is not us carrying anything through,* it is GOD POWER! We just do our work to the best of our ability and let God do the rest. How cool is that! Plus everyone must take responsibility for their own choices and decisions in life. (Remember what was written in the Money book about decision.)

At Level Three or Two this is much harder when our loved ones or business partners start to worry as at these Levels we love so deeply and are VERY sensitive to the energies around us, so we can even become ill, as we desire to have everyone be prosperous and happy and we feel it is all *our* responsibility. Yes, we are responsible to do all we can to the best of our ability and show up and smile and have strong intent but HOW it all works is God's responsibility. God *is* the supplier and God *is* the supply. God is the only Source. When the veil of illusion is lifted, all we truly desire shows up as it was always there.

We live in God's Kingdom, we are offspring to the only power there is. How could we think we control any of it? *We* do not, *I AM* does! God is the only power, not the banks, not people and certainly not our minds. God is the only power there is. God is not even the creator as that would imply that there was a beginning. There has always been Eternity/God just as we have always been and God is always with us, always, even when we do not believe. Oh what a feeling of peace, confidence and gratitude and amazement we have when at Level Four we finally know this to be True. No one can intellectualize Truth; Truth must be experienced from within.

Now we know we are an instrument of Light and yet we are not in complete unity with the Sea where we can say, as Jesus the Christ said, *I AM The Light of The World...* We can feel the Light, but our ego is still healthy enough, as is our humility, to know we are not there yet. If we have to ask if we are there ... well...we are not there, Are *we there yet? I'm thirsty, I'm hungry, I need to go to the loo, are we there yet?* Not yet ...

So now let us now visit the place where so few have traveled Level Five ...

Level Five
I Am The Sea

It is said that if there are 100 Enlightened Ones on the planet at the same time, the world would become instantly awake. Now that there are so many people on our planet there are more and more awakened ones within our midst. Never judge anyone; you may be sitting next to a Buddha on a bus one day...

This is a story that has been told by many over the centuries including by Sri Ramakrishna. I have taken the liberty of changing it a little for this conversation.

There was a little girl completely made of sand, she would sit on the beach and look lovingly out at the Infinite Sea. She wanted very much to go in and swim but she was afraid of the water but then one day she decided to no longer be afraid and go in for a swim. As she reached the waters edge the small waves came up and licked at her feet and she noticed that her feet were dissolving into the water, it tickled and felt good but at the same time it frightened her so she ran back. Again her longing for the Sea was too powerful a desire so she again walked up to the small waves and her feet again started to dissolve into the Sea and it felt so good that she was no longer afraid and loved the feeling so much that she walked into the Sea and dissolved into The Sea of Eternity.

What a beautiful story. This says it all for Level Five. All the ice has melted and we are at last consciously, and completely, One with The Sea Of Eternity. We cannot really call Enlightenment a Level as now there is only The Sea. Enlightened ones no longer live in duality and have become God Conscious. Spiritual Masters who have devoted their lives to giving us Truth have brought us to our present Level of consciousness. The Light that we experience today is the result of the Light which has come down through time from these Enlightened Ones. There are souls teaching us from on high whenever we decide to connect to their Light.

Here are some names you may recognize of these rare beings who have realized that *they are* the Sea of Eternity, a reflection of God-in-form: Saint Francis of Assisi, Jesus the Christ, Sri Ramakrishna, Paramahansa Yogananda, Babaji, Sai Baba, Mother Mira, Mary Magdalene, Joel S. Goldsmith, Mahendra Kumar Trivedi, Shankara, Rama, Saint Teresa of Avila, Braco, Swami Muktananda, Milarepa, Kundalini, Hermes Trismegistus, Lord Buddha...and more that are anonymous. This list continues. This list we have are saints that are alive today and some long ago, but as there truly is no time they are all here now. This list is not that long as there are more Enlightened Ones who have left no record, and yet we still DO enjoy their teachings that have been transmitted esoterically. We *gratefully* thank them ALL as they are all aspects of THE DIVINE, sent here to help bring us h**om**e. (OM)

As mentioned many times during this conversation, we are keeping this book simple so I will not be going into the details of these Enlightened beings lives or their teachings. I have listed recommended books about and from these Masters, these saints, at the end of this book for your further studies.

These rare Enlightened Beings mentioned wrote/write or taught/teach *Truth.* (As time is an illusion that was a challenge to write) Some are with us in form and others appear when necessary, while others have not been seen (That we know about) for thousands of years. We sometimes feel that Enlightened Beings must have only lived thousands of years ago, however IF this world is constantly changing and evolving, then it only makes sense that consciousness is also evolving through us. Plus there is no time. There ARE rare Beings of Enlightenment alive today. Some are still with us in the physical and some we are simply gifted by their Light through their teachings and students. But they are *all* still alive, as we are all immortal and they just knew they were. They had/have become one with the Sea, one with Eternity, One with God. There is no duality. They can say, *I Am The Light. The Grace that was flowing through me is now I... I Am Divine Grace; I Am the Sea of Unlimited Consciousness!*

Some were Avatars like the Maha Avatar, Babaji. Avatars are rare Beings who never lived in physical form here before, they only took on a physical body to help the seekers. Babaji still appears hundreds of years later in real flesh and blood to initiate a new soul to teach. Some became Enlightened through experiencing the many mind states and Levels of consciousness and have had many physical bodies before. Some call Enlightened ones Ascended Masters.

Saint Francis of Assisi woke up from Level One to Level Five whoosh, and people, at first - including his family, thought he had gone mad. Many families and friends of these beings simply think they have lost their minds. *I wonder how many were put away that we do not know of... mmmm...* Anyhow, irrespective of what Enlightenment Level they were at, they *were* way beyond any Level in physical consciousness and way beyond Level Four. It takes a HUGE leap in realization to go from Level Four to Five, although these great Teachers of Light have let us know that it is possible and have gifted us with teachings of Truth, to help us do the same. Jesus the Christ said, *"These works and even greater will you do."*

Not all Enlightened Beings become Teachers with students some only teach esoterically and are purely healers, vessels of Light. Once people realized they were in the presence of Divinity they would come to be healed.

We can tap into their Divinity through contemplating their teachings and meditating on their words. Oh what bliss when we feel their words come to life and we know that we are no longer merely reading words but we are in fact having God's message transmitted through us. Oh what gifts God has given us with these beautiful Enlightened Teachers of Truth. It is almost too much for me to write about these Teachers as I think on all who have helped me on my path that my heart is now overflowing with love, gratitude and wonder! It is ineffable to attempt to describe the magnanimity of these illuminated Teachers of Light. It truly is beyond words.

These Great Ones can help anyone swimming, seeking, as now they are the Sea, waters, the tides and the waves. They no longer live in human ego-personality, even though they will play act any part that will help us to wake up. Many people think Enlightened Teachers aren't human. They think that they sit around all day and only meditate and that they are extremely passive, instead of the strong beings they truly are. They are our Life Guards, Generals, and Gladiators of Light. Humanity has been programmed to believe that their outer behavior should be religious in nature, and that all is peace and harmony. Most Enlightened Teachers can appear to be exactly the opposite especially when they are putting on an act to help a pupil. They are real characters who can appear sometimes to be a little crazy, speaking in riddles, and engage in pursuits that are not always looked upon as *holy*. These beings have transcended time and space and gone beyond the stereotypical okra robe wearing idea we have of Enlightenment, particularly in the West. It is beyond many to think that one who is not from the East could be a teacher of Truth. Why would they not reincarnate in the West where there REALLY is so much need for Light? Of course they do and they are here now. (Thank you God)

Some will, for certain students, put on a personality that is sweet and slightly reserved and at other times for different students be *totally* outrageous and colorful. Whatever personality they put on, one thing is for sure, they are very funny and have great senses of humor and are quite playful. They do not care what we think of them as they love us so much, their mission is only that we wake up to Truth and release our souls from the *Maya.* There are lots of jokes and laughing taking place between them and their students. Whatever is required for us to have Light transmitted to us they will appear in such a way so we can handle all that Divine Power and Light. They are however, pure and innocent as they live in the place where there is no time or space, where there is no good or bad. Just pure Eternal Sea.

I met one teacher, many years ago when I was new to the path, (who was not fully Enlightened but was experiencing Samadhi and was a very high being) who loved his students so deeply, however whenever he did any public events his language was very colorful and his antics on stage quite outrageous that many people would leave his seminars in disgust. He would then turn to all of us who were still in the room and in his wonderful cockney accent say, *"Right, good, now that we have pissed off the ones who were not ready and who still live in judgment, we will begin the teaching".* And then he would become a totally different person who was so loving and deeply compassionate. His eyes would shine with such Light and love on us all. We just knew he had only been putting on an act to release the ones who were not yet ready, as he knew they would only disrupt the lessons with their judgmental vibes and silliness. Being from a rock 'n' roll background I LOVED his outrageous fun personality.

So how do we go from Level Four to Level Five?

Only God knows. It is Grace! All this author knows is that to love God and meditate and dedicate one's life to Truth, Love and Light is all we can do until Eternity takes over. If we are ready to lose our mermaid tails and become one with the Sea, well then it will be so. As mentioned we cannot know while we are still experiencing some duality. Only God in us knows and it will be done if we are ready. YES of course we desire liberation, FREEDOM from the *Maya*. We must simply allow ourselves to desire God and our unity with God more than anything else. We desire this to serve God, attainment is not what it is about anymore, now it is all about FREEDOM and serving God. We have tasted a little of what REAL FREEDOM is at Level Three and Four and now we want liberation. What do we do now? All we can do is love Light/God/Eternity with all of our hearts and serve all others along the way by becoming brighter everyday through mindfulness, kind acts, creating strong bodies and meditation. And if we are very blessed we will meet an Enlightened Teacher who can help us! When we are ready a Teacher will come to us either in human form or in another way. WE simply dissolve into the Light and never come back the same. We are now conduits in an organic body to allow The Divine Light to pour through and heal the world.

There is no one who can explain what Enlightenment is, except of course an Enlightened Soul and then they may say, *It cannot possibly be understood here, in this three-dimensional world you call home.* For those of us who have studied for many years, we may *think* we understand it, but if so we are only allowing our minds to play tricks on us again and may even tell us we are Masters and have already arrived. Our intellectual, so called, understanding of Enlightenment will be a conceptual idea, as Enlightenment resides in world's that are way beyond our conceptual knowledge or intellect.

Lets us now allow Lord Buddha's teaching to help us a little to explain why it cannot be explained. Buddha explained to his disciples *that Enlightenment cannot be explained.* He made it very clear to his students through his discourses on the dharma, *Enlightenment can be attained only through an individual's practice of meditation,* and *that all of the explanations and rituals that are often associated with self discovery will not lead a person to true Enlightenment.* He made it abundantly clear that Enlightenment can be experienced only through the actual practice of meditation. He said, *The more we think we understand Enlightenment, the less we really know it.*

We see, when in an Enlightened Beings presence, gold Light emanating and we feel such exquisite love that we simply *know* we are literally standing in front of God Consciousness. If we are too clogged we may not see or feel a thing but something will have shifted for even the sleepiest sleep walker. Awake Ones, no longer live in human consciousness, yes they have a human vehicle but you know that 24/7 they are God reflecting and beaming Light Source. It is living in the timelessness, no past or future, just NOW!

So let's look into what we have been taught from true Enlightened Teachers as to what they actually experience during the transition period. It has been said that the cells of the person who is transitioning into full God Consciousness are being changed, and infused with Light. This can be painful as this Light is no light that can be experienced on the earth-plane of consciousness. So the person literally, after this period, has cells of Light which is why they radiate gold and explains why some can disappear and appear again wherever they choose.

It can take some many months of integrating themselves into both worlds after Enlightenment has been achieved. Often they require someone to dress and feed them until they are ready to live as God Consciousness in both worlds. (Although they now live in so many dimensions and worlds as the One Sea) This can also happen to some degree during Level Four, as we have such deep Light and spiritual experiences, we can lose ourselves in the Light and may not be even able to speak, let alone drive at certain times, so even at Level Four it helps tremendously to have someone or more than one friend who can be there for us to assist in the assimilation. We do require some help in assimilating to both worlds at Level Four as we come in and out, but this must be nothing in comparison to what is experienced during the transition to Enlightenment.

Some Enlightened Saints do not teach *per se*, as they are in Nirvikalpa-Samadhi most of the time and they have to have people feed them and look after them, because their bodies just can't be experienced. One of this author's deep loves and Teachers is Sri Ramakrishna. When first reading his words I was literally overcome with joy and love. I had to choose times when I could read his teachings as I knew when I did I would be good for nothing else for the rest of the day. Sri Ramakrishna went into Nirvikalpa- Samadhi at the drop of a hat and he had to be looked after and have someone with him at all times so that he would not hurt himself when he walked as he was no longer here. You see why we have to have strong bodies and minds as even at Level Four the Light is so intense we have to learn how to ground ourselves. Sri Ramakrishna, I feel was born an Avatar! An avatar has not been here before they just come to earth to help us from the kindness and strength of God. They are completely God Consciousness. There is NO duality at all in an Avatar.

Some souls have decided to come back in a particular time in history as Light was needed to wake people up from so much darkness. These Beings come and teach many things, including how to become very successful in our careers so that we can then have the freedom required to live fully. Money does have power per say but it can gift to us the freedom to live an independent dedicated, giving life.

When we read an Enlightened Teachers Truth we *feel it* within our very being. We reach a certain Level of awareness where we just *feel* and *know* that this person is one with God. It does not matter whether we *see* anything, if we are *feeling* it is all beautiful, it is a knowing that Divinity wrote those words, or perhaps, is standing right in front of us at the post office in the form of a small child.

Now we have come to the end of this conversation however for you it can be the beginning...We are all souls. We are beautiful luminous souls experiencing this amazing world. So whatever needs to be done to help the souls and our own soul *is* being done and we can *always* trust that.

May the glorious, giving, generous, Holy Light of Eternity Bless Your LIFE! It has been a great honor to have this time together; I wish you boundless joy on your path, overflowing with Peace, Light, Blessings and Abundance.

The Sea of Pure Light is waiting to take you home to...FREED-OM

THE MYSTICAL SUCCESS CLUB™
www.MysticalSuccessClub.com

**Vibrate at a higher frequency.
Ignite Your True Unlimited Potential and Experience Success in Life Through Transformation of Consciousness with this life changing platform.
Since 2003 transforming thousands of lives.**

The Mystical Success Club™

How can we transform our lives?

Through transforming our consciousness. Can we do this alone? Yes, however it is a very difficult path to do alone. Here at the Mystical Success Club you are prayed for every single day and sent transmissions of Light Energy (Shakti).

Here in the Mystical Success Club it is our goal and positive intention to strip away old paradigms of false beliefs and become one with our true Higher Self. And hence our Divine Destiny is at last revealed in all its glory! There is much given through this membership in Divine vibrational energy transmissions, exercises, monthly DVDs and more.

Do you wish to have harmony, happiness and fulfilling success? You can wake up to who you truly are. ALL things are possible. The natural evolution for all sentient beings and that means YOU, is ENLIGHTENMENT! If you feel you want evolution in all areas of you life then watch our FREE videos at...

www.MysticalSuccessClub.com/video

What others are saying...

"Michele Blood is truly a special person. For over three decades, I have made serious study of the mind and how to live a full and balanced life. I have taught tens of thousands of people around the world how to properly utilize their God-given potential, and then along came Michele Blood. She had a very positive impact on my life, for which I am truly grateful! She made me aware of unique methods for realizing more power by effectively combining affirmations and music. Invest in her entire library and let this petite powerhouse show you a fast and effective way to enjoy more of life's rich rewards. I enthusiastically introduce Michele Blood and her wonderful work to every audience. Order her material today! Share Michele and MusiVation™ discovery with your world; they will thank you with sincere gratitude." **- Bob Proctor, Author of the Best Selling Book "You Were Born Rich"**

Michele belongs in every achiever's library.
- Samuel A. Cypert, Author of "Achieve & Believe"

Dearest Michele, I want to say Thank You So Much for all that you're doing for the Mystical Club Members. You've made my life alive again. Thank you, Thank you...- **Patti C**

Being introduced to Michele's Mystical Success Club my life has changed for the best. I can get the most powerful, up-lifting and energizing emotions when I participate in any of Michele's in-person or Weimar sessions. My life has been so hectic over the past few months, but I make it my priority to spend time listening and learning from Michele, because she brings my life back into absolute consciousness. I appreciate and treasure the time Michele dedicates to helping those who are searching for their higher self. I absolutely feel I achieve a higher consciousness with each and every one of Michele's sessions. Thank you, thank you, thank you…. I am gaining momentum to my higher self, to reaching my unlimited consciousness. God Bless You Michele. - **Don Runowski.**

When Michele first prayed for me and gave me specific instructions to feel the stillness within I was in over $500,000 credit card debt in just 4 months I was out of debt through a totally unexpected gift. I feel free and happy and am now also in a new Beautiful relationship with someone who really gets me. - **J'En El Author/speaker**

I am blown away with Michele's enthusiasm and genuine energy she is able to project. I have followed her work and Bob Proctors for years. In the past year I received and email about a seminar she was holding and I attended and was blown away. It seemed to fit into everything I had always known the theory of what my own mystical projects were about. Now I'm a member of her Mystical Success Club with ongoing Light Transmissions, monthly DVD's and weekly webinars. I find this a rare way to evolve and to stay current. This club is helping me stay true to purpose, direction; I am growing in knowledge and light experience with someone who has years of success as an author, mentor, musician, career coach, and mystic etc. and I LOVE IT! Thank you Michele! **- Kim Ripley Hartt Author of Mysticism**

Michele's insights, music and exploration into the mystical success we can tap into through her club and many other products and books takes all that she has to offer to help with the richness of her transformational teachings. I loved the club and the monthly DVD's are pouring with energy transmission. I highly recommend it as a priceless sacred space for you to grow in consciousness and to bring harmony to all of your family members. **- Bernadette Dimitrov Author for Children's books**

Dear Michele, It is with a heart full of gratitude that I am writing this email tonight. I've just finished watching the meditation DVD, and for that I am grateful. Your face shines because of the Love and Gratitude that you have for the Divine/God. And your Prayer recording also made a major shift in my heart. The words cannot describe how grateful I am to have found you when I did. My prayers to God were to end my life if I had to continue living the same way. For without God in my life, I am nothing. And I forgot to listen to my heart and more importantly I forgot the main ingredient: GRATITUDE. You have opened my eyes as to why I lost my Faith. And dear Michele I have to thank you for having restored my Faith in the Divine/God. I have re-gained something priceless: my Faith. It is so true that in every minute of our lives, we have to choose thoughts that will determine our future. **- J Marie**

A quick note Michele to let you know that I had one of the best weeks in a long time. I am on a very large global computer system project that has a lot of negative energy associated with it because of the perceived time constraints with the amount of work to do. Many of the people on this project are frustrated which I was one of them until this past week. I believe it was the prayer you did for me last Saturday that changed my energy levels and something else in me. I am at peace, energized and very positive knowing things will work out. A big change from where I used to operate because I worried, stressed on time deadlines for many years. It lets me think more clearly now, probably more creative but it has only been a week. I feel transformed. **- Gary B**

Thank you so much Michelle. You did prayers for me last Christmas and almost everything came true!! It has been a blessed year. **- L Cash**

Michele, The Mystical Success Club and your prayers have done SO MUCH for my life! There has been so much I appreciate of all of your work and love. Being part of this club had healed so many wounds that my past had left me with, and it has allowed me to move forward so much in bravery and perseverance. As a member, I feel so honored to be part of such beautiful love. Never in my life have I felt so close to a circle of such open and loving people. Being part of the mystical path had broken so many of the restricting chains of resistance I had. I was caught up in a mess of a depression so painful I had lost almost all sanity, yet something just kept telling me "Keep strong and keep believing, what you're looking for is just around the corner". . I knew this was where true light was and what it really meant to feel freedom. Or rather FREED- OMMMMMMM! I can't seem to find any words to describe this feeling. Thank you Michele for every single thing you've given me. Thank you, thank you, thank you, and may you be blessed with all of my love. Thank you. I LOVE YOU!
- Eleida N Y

Michele, I wanted to thank you again for who you are and what you do. God has given to the world a special gift with you. He is truly working through you. It's been about two weeks now since I was on the special prayer call that you opened up to many people. Thank you for doing that! Since then I have joined the Mystical Success club, I continue to live each day with much more joy and happiness and I know I am just beginning my way to being one with the universe in consciousness, one with everyone and everything. I feel like I am being reborn and my consciousness is awakening. I have been living unconsciously almost my whole life, although I knew there was something waiting to bust out but didn't know how to do it. I know God wants to use me and I yearn for that. He has brought me to you to make this happen. Lots of Energy and Love. **- George B**

Dear Michele, Your prayers helped me to find a job working with developmentally disabled Souls. So many Miracles! Bless you so much! With Love and Light. **- Caroline**

Thank you, Michele, since I joined the MSClub I've been feeling my heart open more and more, thank you for that! I want to share something with

you, it's an experience that filled my being with joy. Today, I was walking down the street, thinking about something you said on one of the weekly webinars — you said that there is logic language, and then there is love language. And there and then, I realized — love language is wordless! It's everything, and everywhere, it's all around me! It's the trees standing by the roadside, it's the air around us, its people, unconnected, all over the world, just doing anything — walking, sleeping, eating, breathing... I am love language, I am love language speaking itself through me. Even logic language is love, it is not apart from it, it couldn't exist if not for love! All of this, all of us, we are the language of love. And it is being spoken, all the time, everyday.... I couldn't not speak it. I couldn't not hear it. Thank you for giving me this experience, it is this that I have been yearning for so long. I knew I knew this someplace, somewhere, I had just forgotten for a little while.
- **Yen L**

I just wanted to tell you that I have received what I asked for in the prayer request I sent you and to tell you what happened, it is very interesting! I had sent in a request prayer for my sister Diane to find a job and a place to live (they were staying with me since they moved to CA) Well Michele, today they picked up the keys to their apartment and will be moving within this week! My prayer was answered! - **Vicky W**

My dear Michele, Thank you very much for your priceless energy transformation. Since Sunday my husband has been transforming in a good way. After a really long time he is interested in me again and hugs me kisses me and I can see the love in his eyes. This is like miracle and how much I appreciate your help!!! Thank you very much again for all your help. God bless you. - **Yonca**

Dearest Angel Michele. Very fast miracle after your Light Transmission. The transfer I wanted to Kochin City came in 20 hours later. It's incredibly beautiful. It has to be felt to be believed. I am grateful for your kind blessed light. Improved my health also. Thanking your beautiful soul. Tour energy par compare. - **Sreekanth – India**

FULL 8 CD Audio version of this Powerful book spoken by the authors with added extras is available at
www.MusiVation.com

This powerful audio book that people are raving about is also available as downloadable MP3 audio files on our e site
www.EMusiVation.com

Or from Amazon.com, Barnes & Noble, Borders and all good bookstores worldwide!
For wholesale orders of this book
Call USA (1) (858) 268-8688

Our MAIN WEBSITES

To book Michele Blood and Bob Proctor for your next event or to train your company goes to...
www.BobProctor.com and www.MicheleBlood.com

www.MysticalSuccessClub.com

For all of the Musivation books, DVD's and Positive Mind Changing Music go to www.MusiVation.com

www.EMusiVation.com
E site for product immediate success product downloads including Bob Proctor and other Teachings.

www.BeAMagnetToMoney.com

By Masters In Consciousness

MASTERY AT WORK
18 Keys for Achieving Success, Fulfillment
and Joy In Any Profession
and
BODHISATTVA: How To Be Free
unfolds secret teachings of the High Dharma
by Nicole Grace

THE PROPHET
By Kahil Gibran

JONATHAN LIVINGSTON SEAGULL
By Richard Bach

A PARENTHESIS In ETERNITY
By Joel S. Goldsmith

THE PISTIS SOPHIA
A Gnostic Gospel
G.R.S. Mead

ISLAND
By Aldous Huxley

The Bible
Particularly St John in the New Testament

THE SCIENCE OF BEING GREAT
By Wallace D. Wattles
(audio version on www.EMusiVation.com)
THE SCIENCE OF BEING RICH
By Wallace D. Wattles
(audio version on www.EMusiVation.com)

RAMAKRISHNA And His Disciples
by
Christopher Isherwood

SHANKARA'S Crest-Jewel of Discrimination
Translated by

Swami Prabhavananda & Christopher Isherwood

INTERIOR CASTLE
Saint Teresa of Avila

BHAGAVAD GITA: The Song of God
Translated By
Swami Prabhavananda & Christopher Isherwood

AUTOBIOGRAPHY of A YOGI
by
Paramahansa Yogananda

THE DHAMMAPADA
Teachings of The Buddha

RAMAYANA
Retold By
William Buck

SIDDARTHA
by
Hermann Hesse

SRIMAD BHAGAVATAM
The Wisdom Of God

THE WAY OF LIFE
According to LAOTZU
Translated by
Witter Bynner

THE TIBETAN BOOK OF LIVING AND DYING
By
Sogyal Rinpoche

HOW TO BE A SUCCESS
By
Paramhansa YOGANANDA

Also look at other friends and amazing Enlightened Ones through their websites

www.BracoAmerica.com

www.TrivediMasterWellness.com

www.LikeSwans.com